JAN 1 5

JR. GRAPHIC GHOST STORIES

THE MAID OF THE MIST

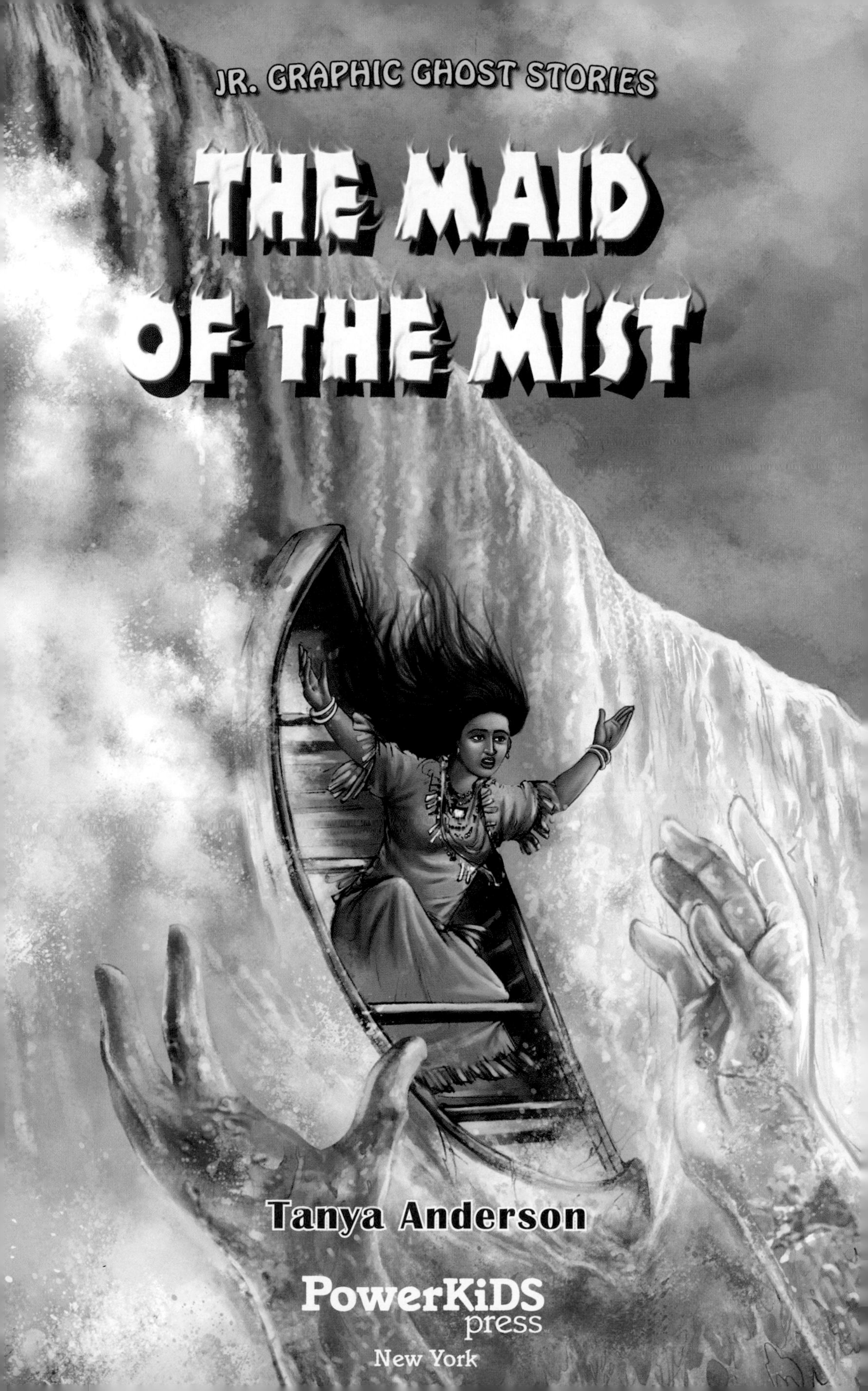

Tanya Anderson

PowerKiDS press
New York

Published in 2015 by The Rosen Publishing Group, Inc.
29 East 21st Street, New York, NY 10010

First Edition

Editor: Joanne Randolph
Book Design: Contentra Technologies
Illustrations: Contentra Technologies

Publisher's Cataloging Data

Anderson, Tanya.

The Maid of the Mist / by Tanya Anderson — first edition.

p. cm. — (Jr. graphic ghost stories)

Includes index.

ISBN 978-1-4777-7129-7 (library binding) — ISBN 978-1-4777-7130-3 (pbk.) — ISBN 978-1-4777-7131-0 (6-pack)

1. Indians of North America — Folklore — Juvenile literature. 2. Folklore — Juvenile literature. I. Anderson, Tanya. II. Title.

E98.F6 A55 2015

398—d23

Manufactured in the United States of America

CPSIA Compliance Information: Batch #WS14PK2: For Further Information contact Rosen Publishing, New York, New York at 1-800-237-9932

Contents

Introduction

You have likely heard of Niagara Falls. There are actually three waterfalls that make up Niagara Falls. Two of them, American Falls and Bridal Veil Falls, are within the United States, and the third, Horseshoe Falls, is on the Canadian side of the border. When most people picture Niagara Falls, they envision Horseshoe Falls, which is the largest and highest of the three. The region around the falls was inhabited by Native Americans centuries before Europeans settled in the area. Over the years, Native American legends about the falls have been told and retold, including this one about a young woman who is transformed into a Thunder Being.

Main Characters

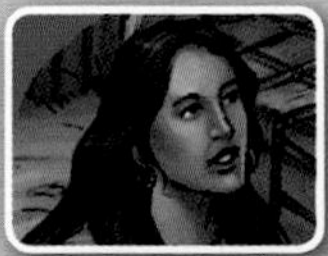

Lelawala Legendary Iroquois/**Ongiara** woman who, in intense grief, went over Niagara Falls in a **canoe** in an effort to commit suicide.

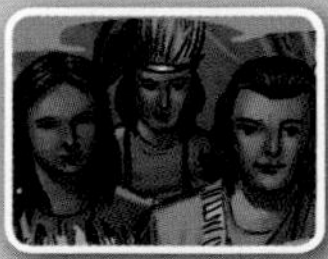

Thunder Beings Native American **spirit** beings who lived under Niagara Falls and later lived in the heavens.

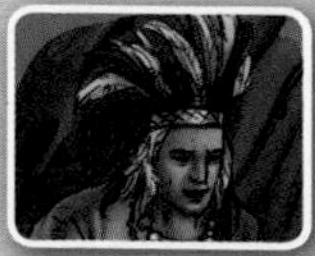

Heno The chief Thunder Being and main god of the skies and storms.

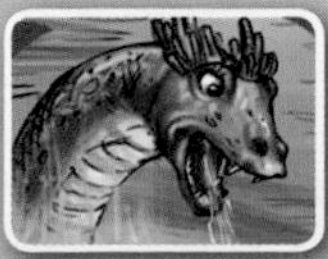

Great Serpent A Native American evil spirit that poisoned people and ate the dead.

The Maid of the Mist

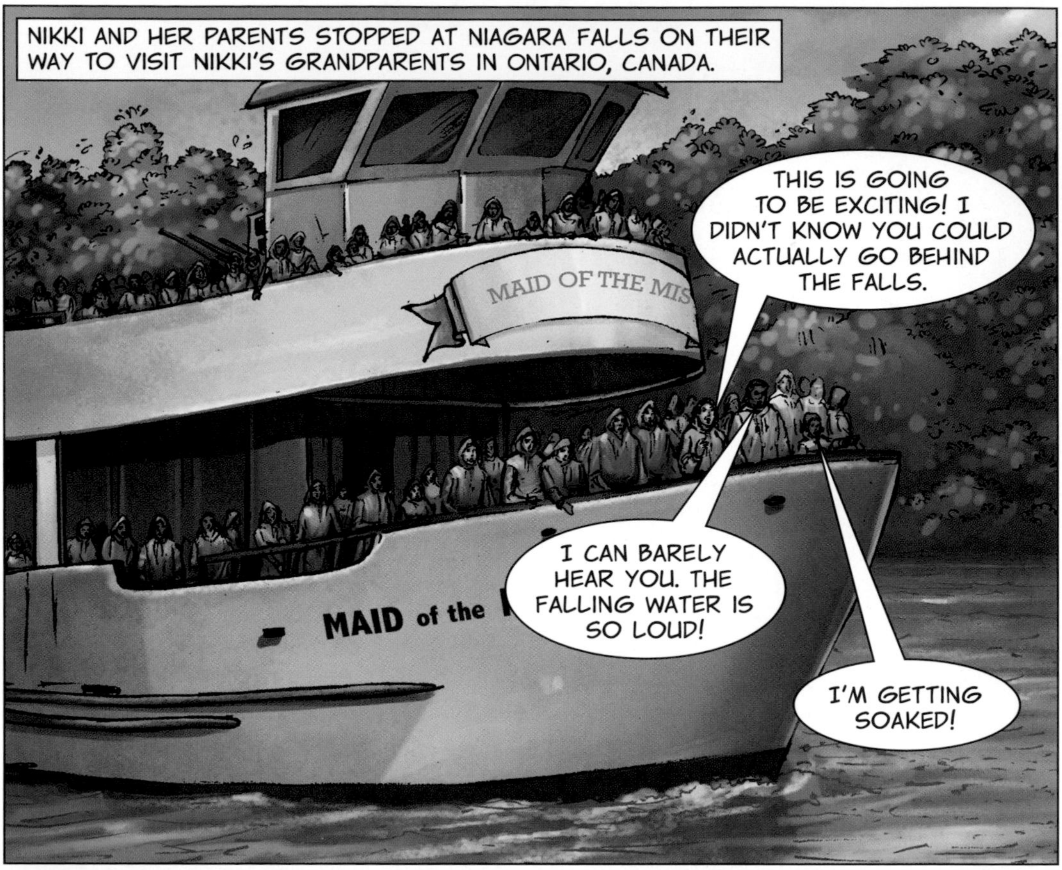
NIKKI AND HER PARENTS STOPPED AT NIAGARA FALLS ON THEIR WAY TO VISIT NIKKI'S GRANDPARENTS IN ONTARIO, CANADA.
THIS IS GOING TO BE EXCITING! I DIDN'T KNOW YOU COULD ACTUALLY GO BEHIND THE FALLS.
I CAN BARELY HEAR YOU. THE FALLING WATER IS SO LOUD!
I'M GETTING SOAKED!

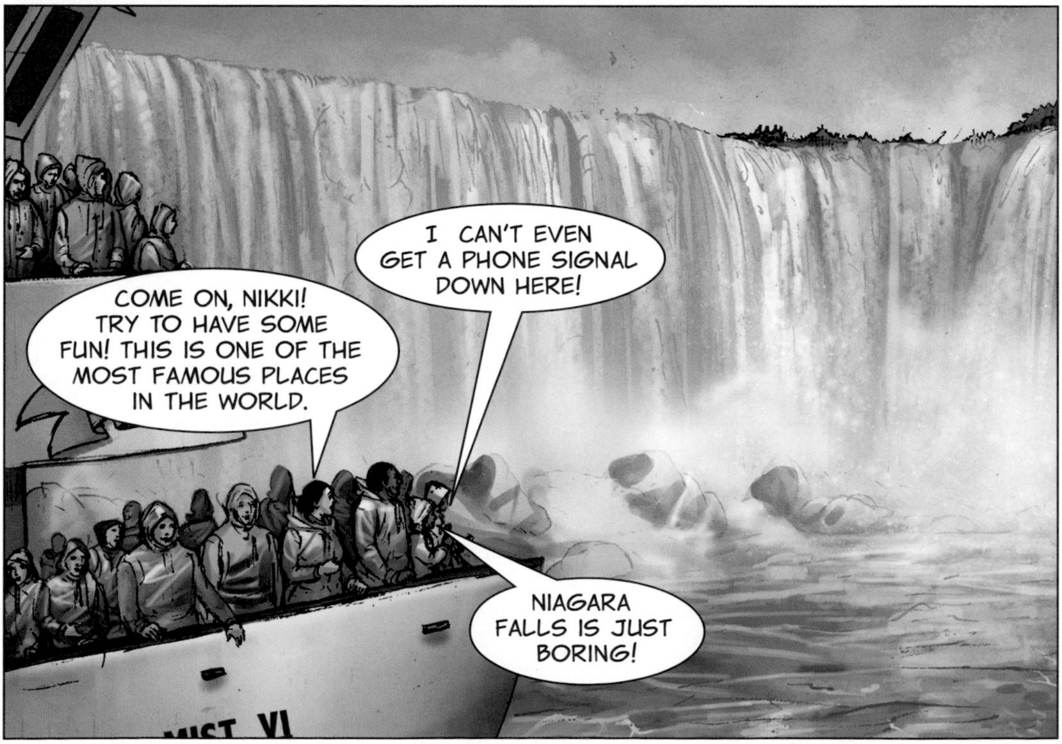
I CAN'T EVEN GET A PHONE SIGNAL DOWN HERE!
COME ON, NIKKI! TRY TO HAVE SOME FUN! THIS IS ONE OF THE MOST FAMOUS PLACES IN THE WORLD.
NIAGARA FALLS IS JUST BORING!

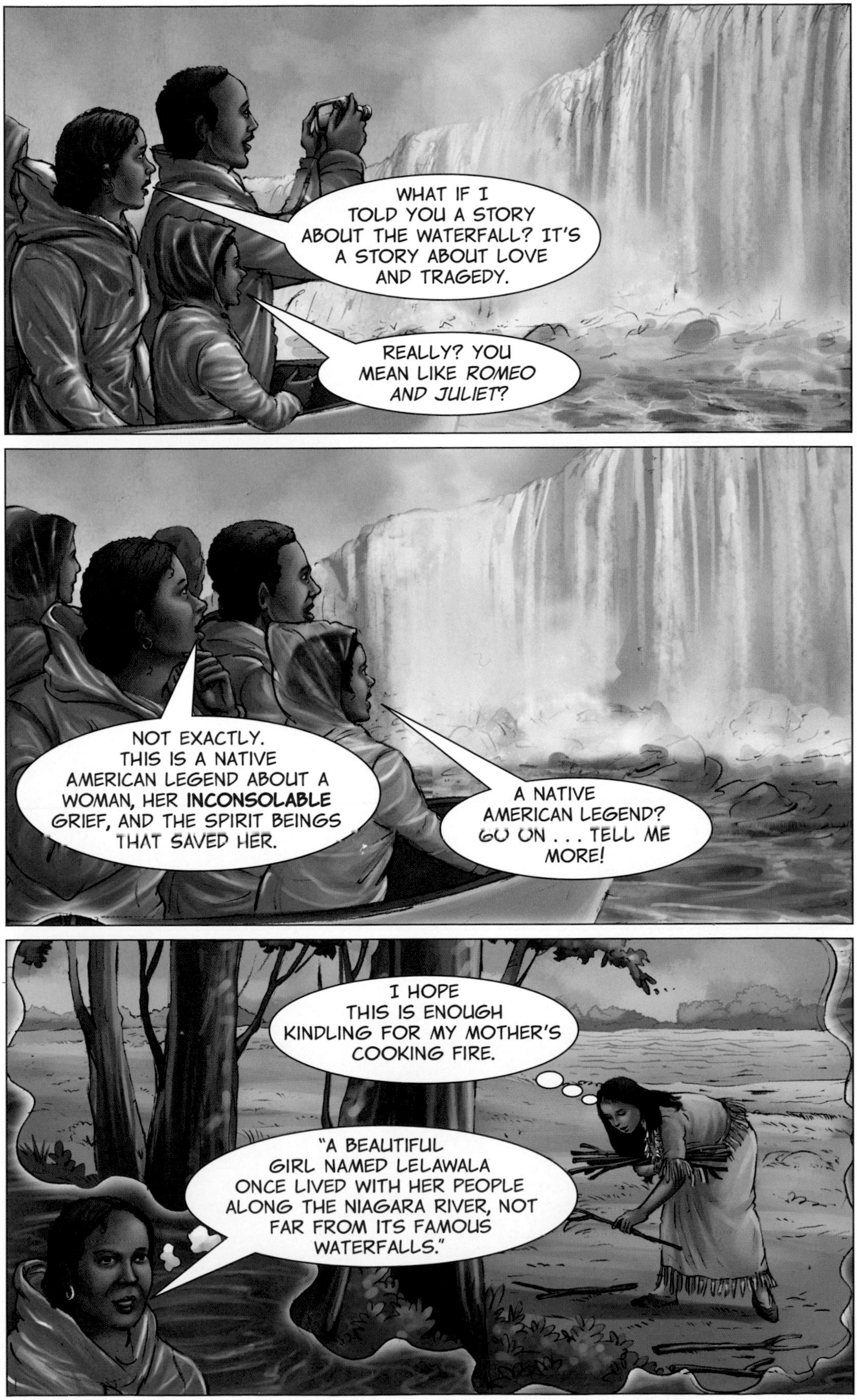
WHAT IF I TOLD YOU A STORY ABOUT THE WATERFALL? IT'S A STORY ABOUT LOVE AND TRAGEDY.
REALLY? YOU MEAN LIKE ROMEO AND JULIET?
NOT EXACTLY. THIS IS A NATIVE AMERICAN LEGEND ABOUT A WOMAN, HER INCONSOLABLE GRIEF, AND THE SPIRIT BEINGS THAT SAVED HER.
A NATIVE AMERICAN LEGEND? GO ON . . . TELL ME MORE!
I HOPE THIS IS ENOUGH KINDLING FOR MY MOTHER'S COOKING FIRE.
"A BEAUTIFUL GIRL NAMED LELAWALA ONCE LIVED WITH HER PEOPLE ALONG THE NIAGARA RIVER, NOT FAR FROM ITS FAMOUS WATERFALLS."

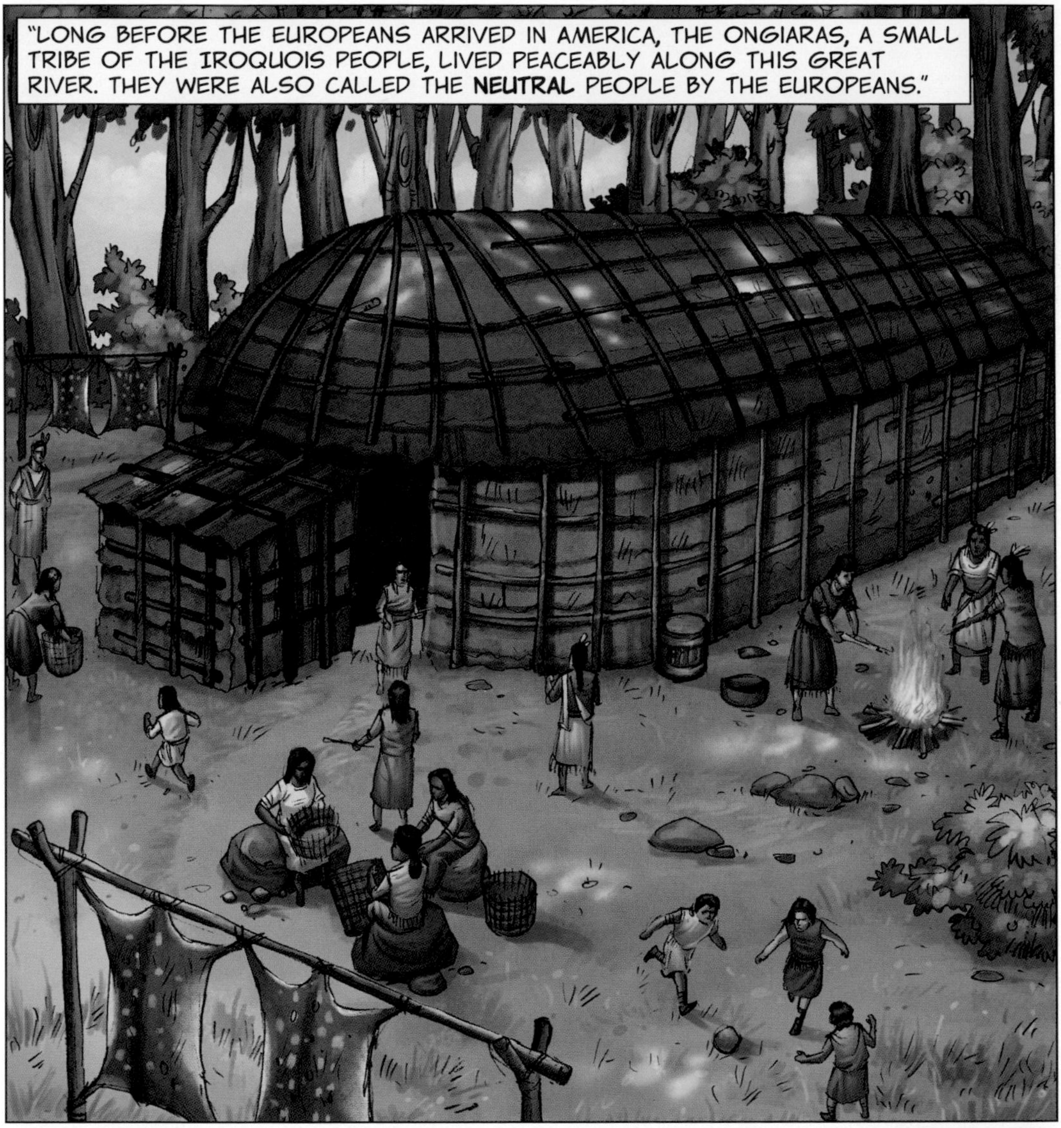
"LONG BEFORE THE EUROPEANS ARRIVED IN AMERICA, THE ONGIARAS, A SMALL TRIBE OF THE IROQUOIS PEOPLE, LIVED PEACEABLY ALONG THIS GREAT RIVER. THEY WERE ALSO CALLED THE **NEUTRAL** PEOPLE BY THE EUROPEANS."

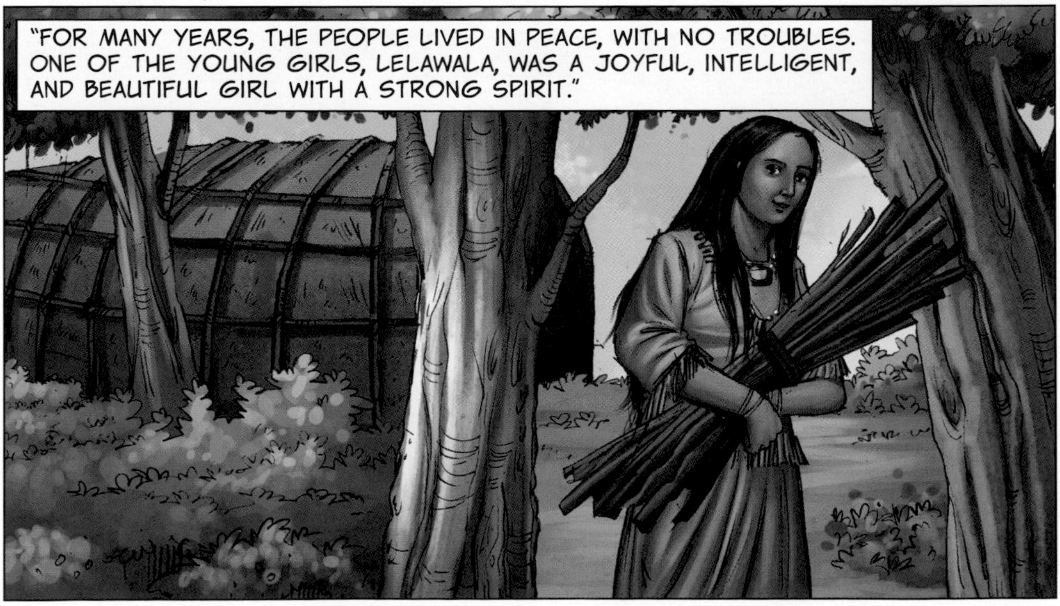
"FOR MANY YEARS, THE PEOPLE LIVED IN PEACE, WITH NO TROUBLES. ONE OF THE YOUNG GIRLS, LELAWALA, WAS A JOYFUL, INTELLIGENT, AND BEAUTIFUL GIRL WITH A STRONG SPIRIT."

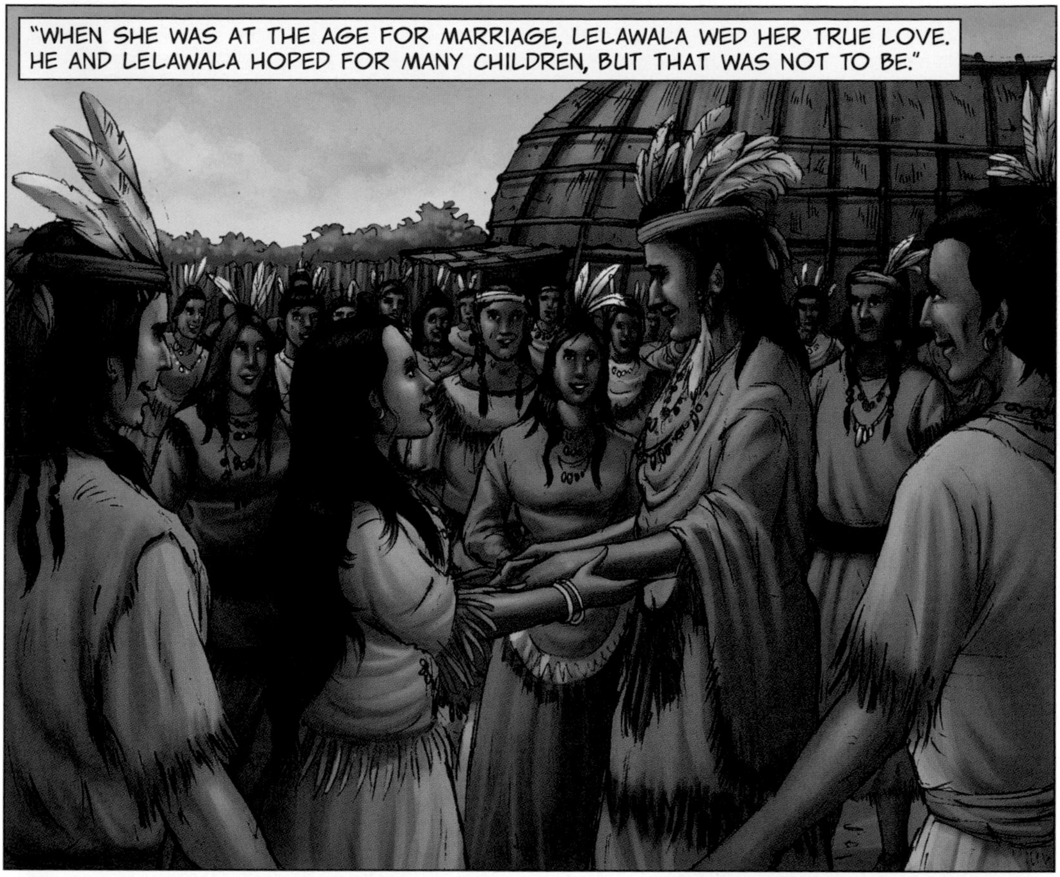
"WHEN SHE WAS AT THE AGE FOR MARRIAGE, LELAWALA WED HER TRUE LOVE. HE AND LELAWALA HOPED FOR MANY CHILDREN, BUT THAT WAS NOT TO BE."

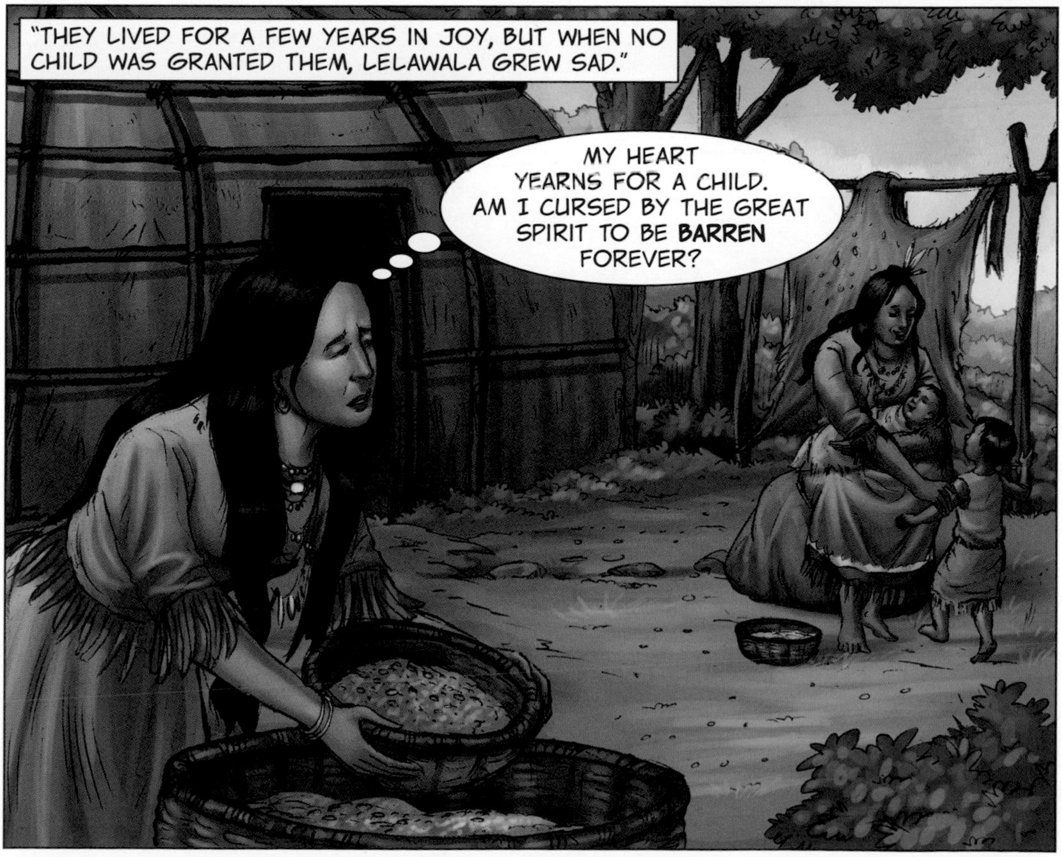
"THEY LIVED FOR A FEW YEARS IN JOY, BUT WHEN NO CHILD WAS GRANTED THEM, LELAWALA GREW SAD."
MY HEART YEARNS FOR A CHILD. AM I CURSED BY THE GREAT SPIRIT TO BE **BARREN** FOREVER?

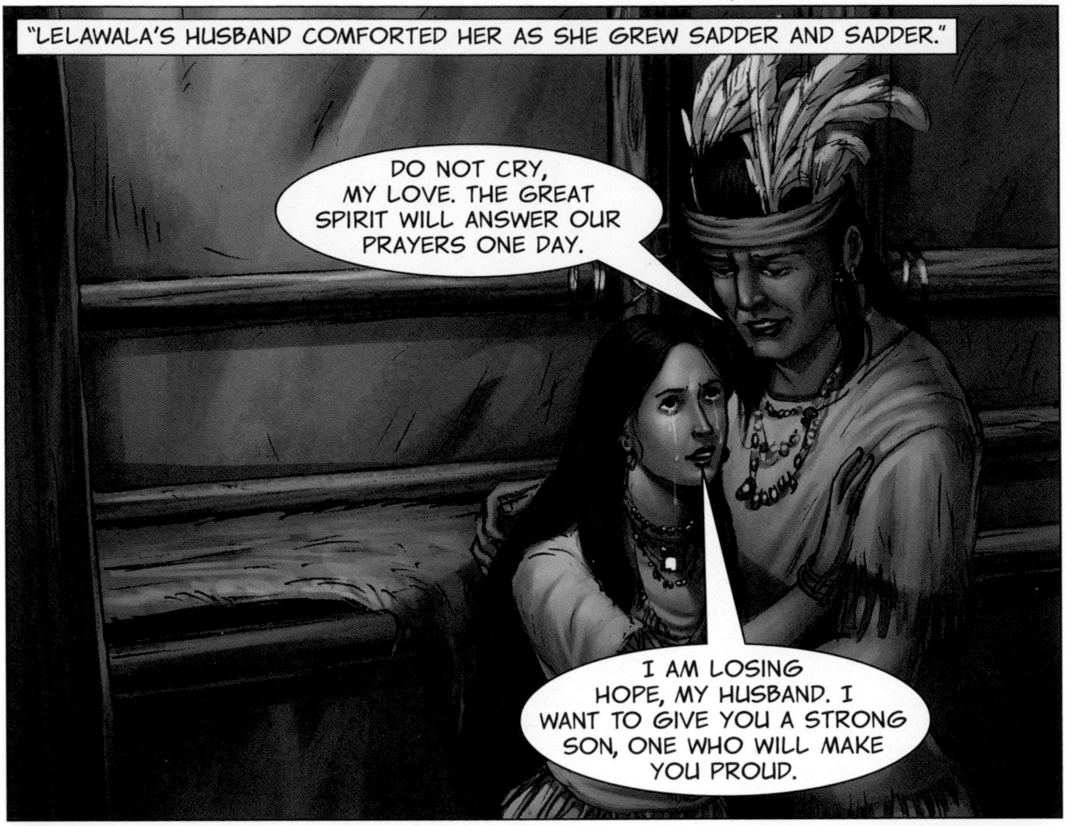
"LELAWALA'S HUSBAND COMFORTED HER AS SHE GREW SADDER AND SADDER."
DO NOT CRY, MY LOVE. THE GREAT SPIRIT WILL ANSWER OUR PRAYERS ONE DAY.
I AM LOSING HOPE, MY HUSBAND. I WANT TO GIVE YOU A STRONG SON, ONE WHO WILL MAKE YOU PROUD.

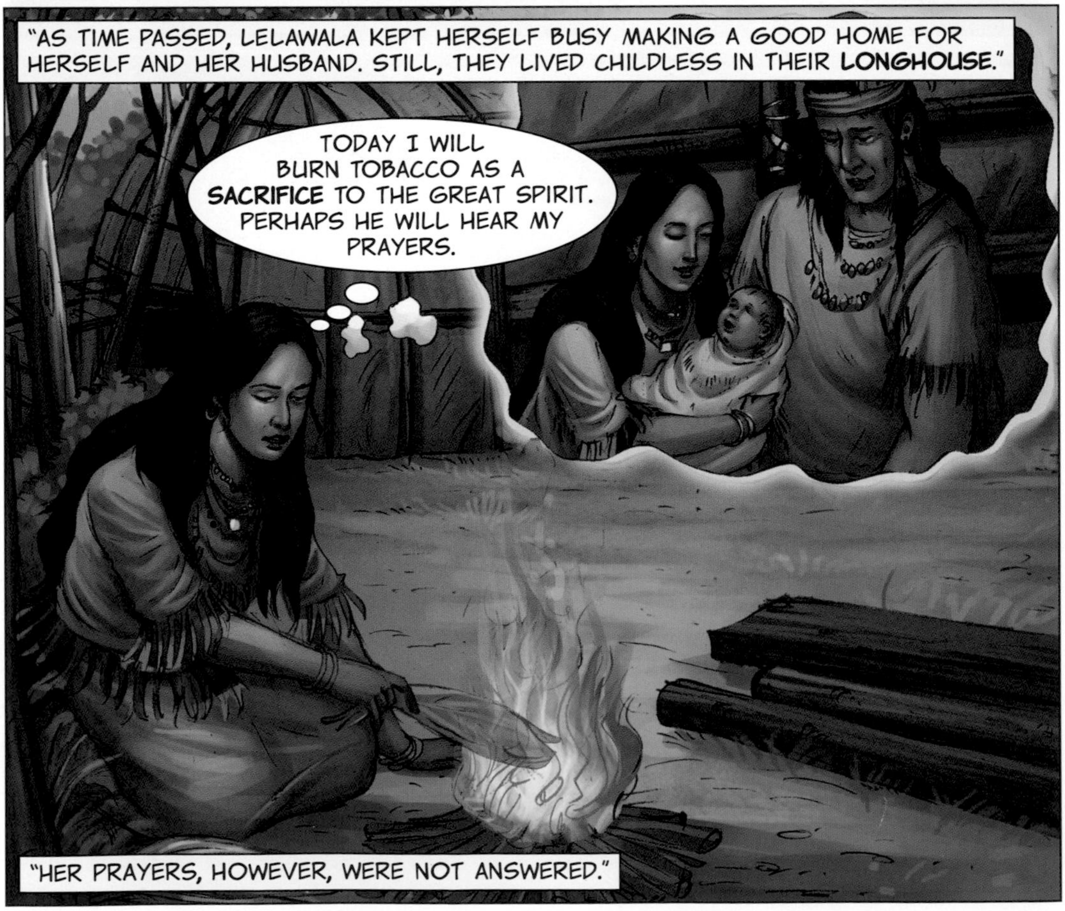
"AS TIME PASSED, LELAWALA KEPT HERSELF BUSY MAKING A GOOD HOME FOR HERSELF AND HER HUSBAND. STILL, THEY LIVED CHILDLESS IN THEIR **LONGHOUSE**."
TODAY I WILL BURN TOBACCO AS A **SACRIFICE** TO THE GREAT SPIRIT. PERHAPS HE WILL HEAR MY PRAYERS.
"HER PRAYERS, HOWEVER, WERE NOT ANSWERED."

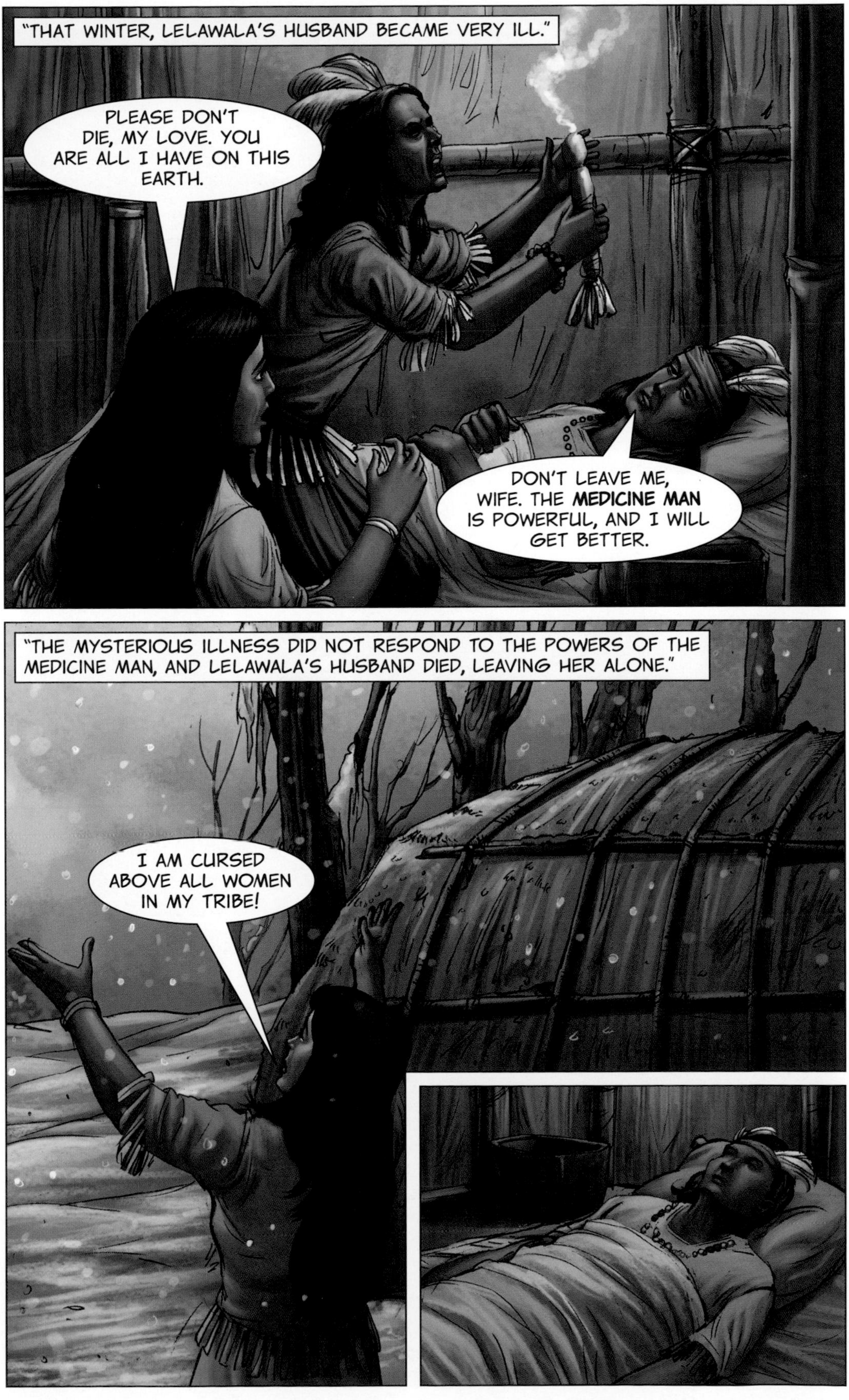
"THAT WINTER, LELAWALA'S HUSBAND BECAME VERY ILL."
PLEASE DON'T DIE, MY LOVE. YOU ARE ALL I HAVE ON THIS EARTH.
DON'T LEAVE ME, WIFE. THE **MEDICINE MAN** IS POWERFUL, AND I WILL GET BETTER.
"THE MYSTERIOUS ILLNESS DID NOT RESPOND TO THE POWERS OF THE MEDICINE MAN, AND LELAWALA'S HUSBAND DIED, LEAVING HER ALONE."
I AM CURSED ABOVE ALL WOMEN IN MY TRIBE!

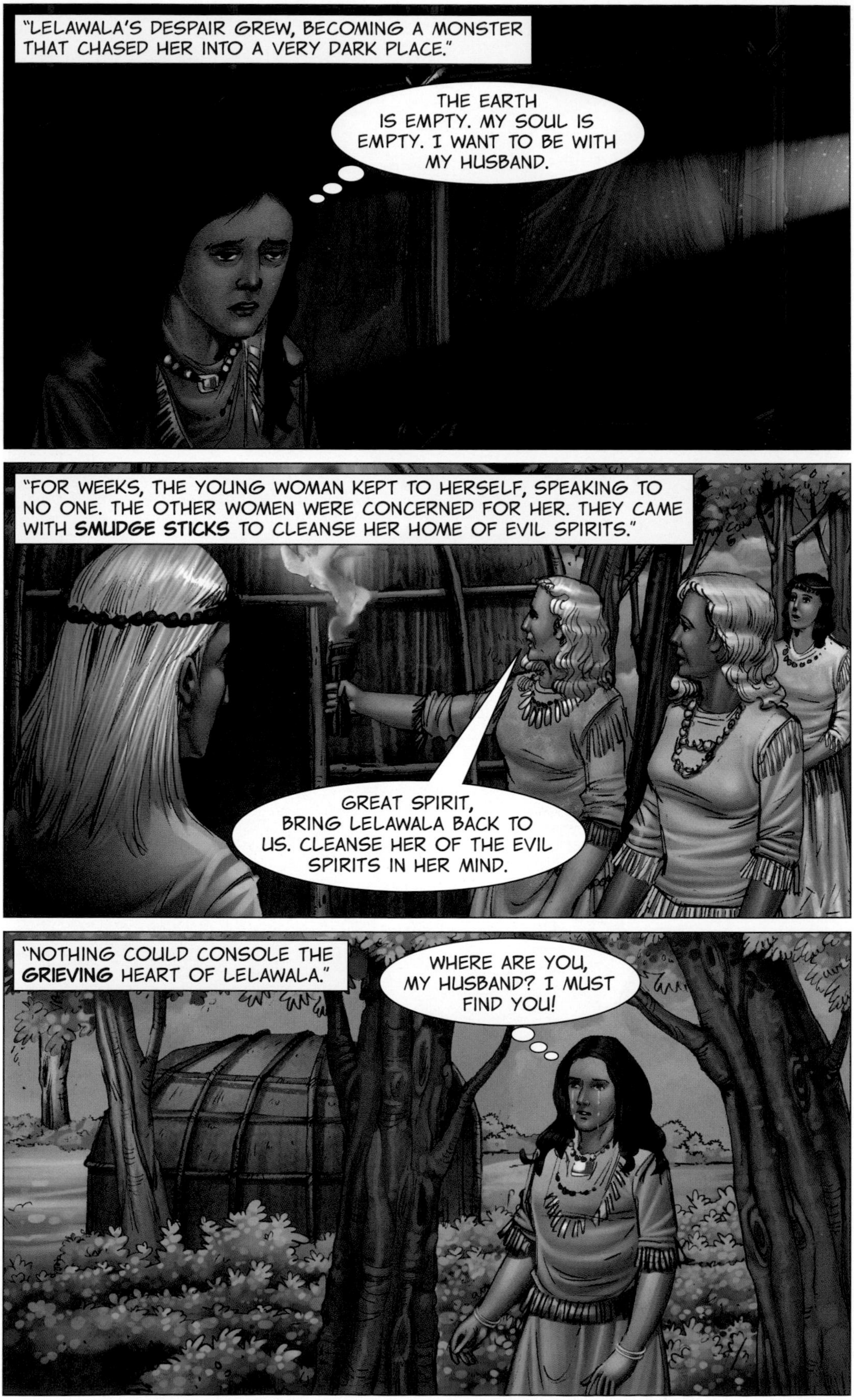
"LELAWALA'S DESPAIR GREW, BECOMING A MONSTER THAT CHASED HER INTO A VERY DARK PLACE."
THE EARTH IS EMPTY. MY SOUL IS EMPTY. I WANT TO BE WITH MY HUSBAND.
"FOR WEEKS, THE YOUNG WOMAN KEPT TO HERSELF, SPEAKING TO NO ONE. THE OTHER WOMEN WERE CONCERNED FOR HER. THEY CAME WITH SMUDGE STICKS TO CLEANSE HER HOME OF EVIL SPIRITS."
GREAT SPIRIT, BRING LELAWALA BACK TO US. CLEANSE HER OF THE EVIL SPIRITS IN HER MIND.
"NOTHING COULD CONSOLE THE GRIEVING HEART OF LELAWALA."
WHERE ARE YOU, MY HUSBAND? I MUST FIND YOU!

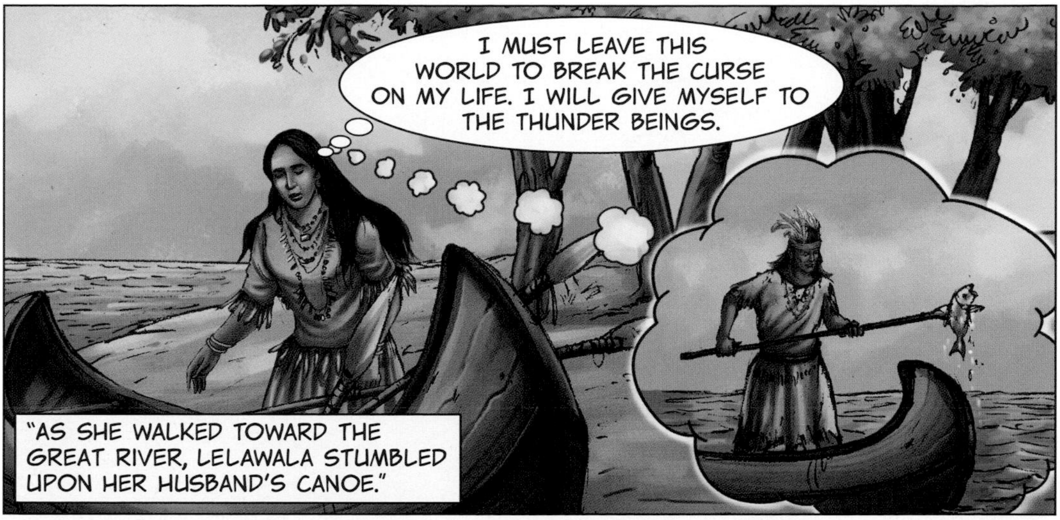
I MUST LEAVE THIS WORLD TO BREAK THE CURSE ON MY LIFE. I WILL GIVE MYSELF TO THE THUNDER BEINGS.
"AS SHE WALKED TOWARD THE GREAT RIVER, LELAWALA STUMBLED UPON HER HUSBAND'S CANOE."

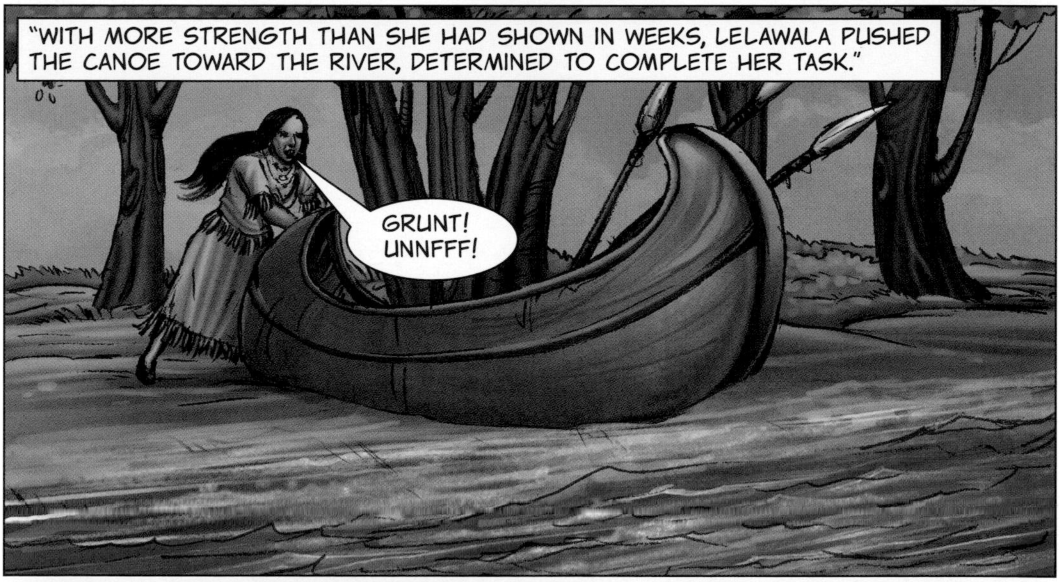
"WITH MORE STRENGTH THAN SHE HAD SHOWN IN WEEKS, LELAWALA PUSHED THE CANOE TOWARD THE RIVER, DETERMINED TO COMPLETE HER TASK."
GRUNT! UNNFFF!

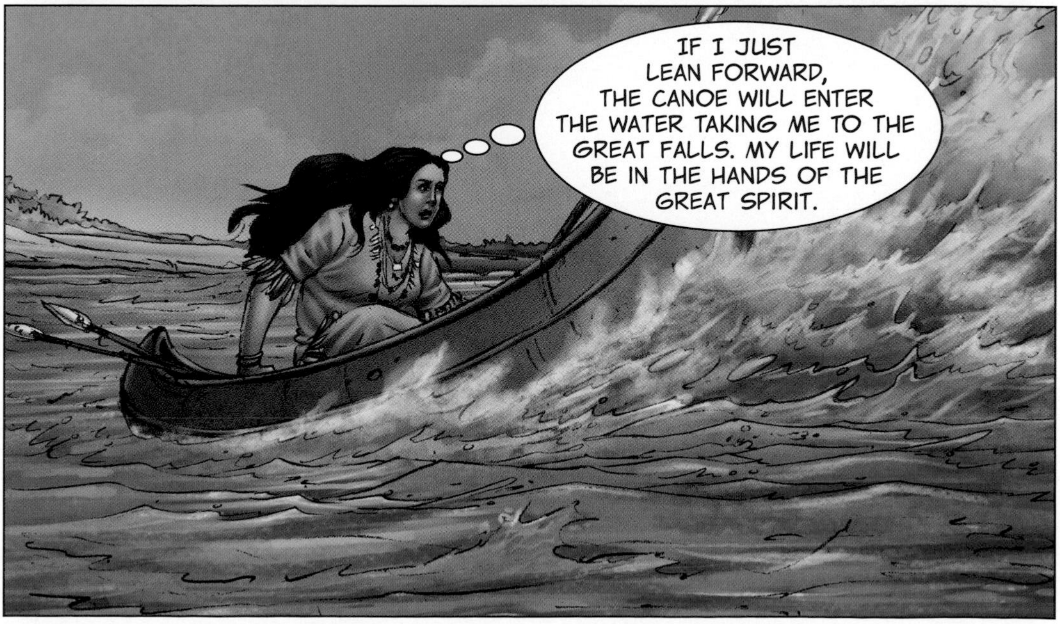
IF I JUST LEAN FORWARD, THE CANOE WILL ENTER THE WATER TAKING ME TO THE GREAT FALLS. MY LIFE WILL BE IN THE HANDS OF THE GREAT SPIRIT.

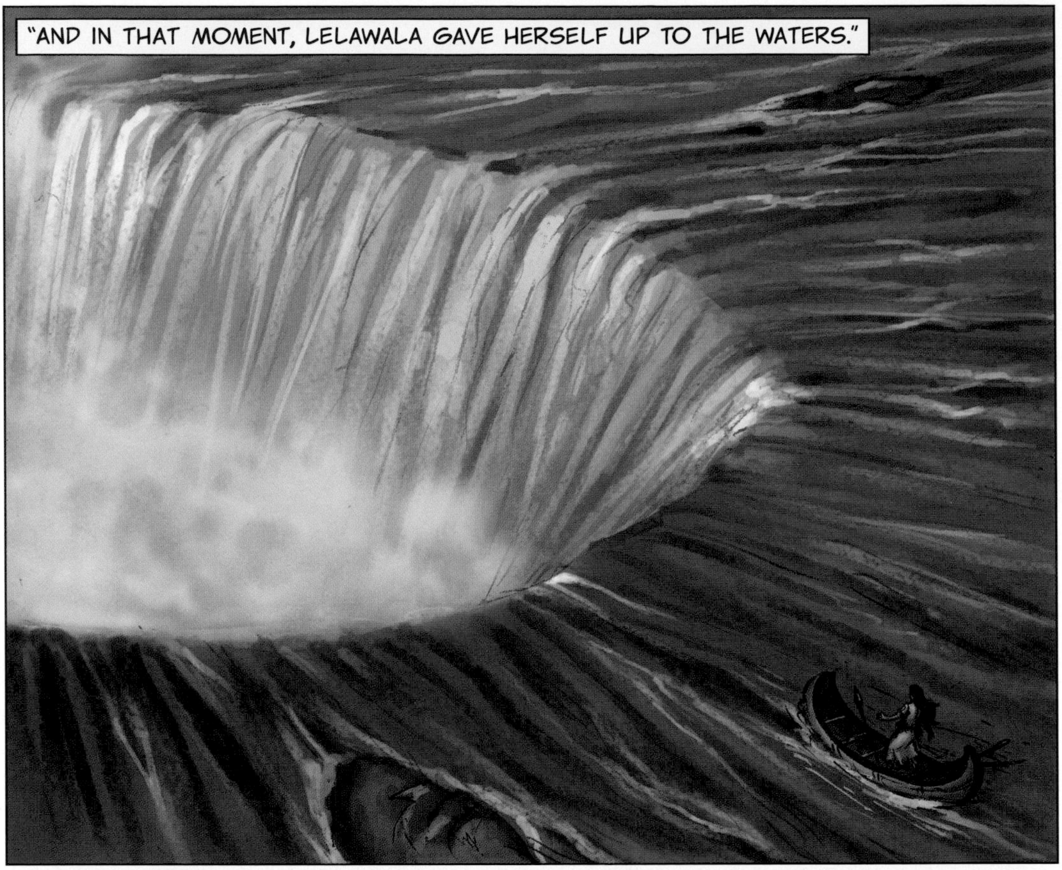
"AND IN THAT MOMENT, LELAWALA GAVE HERSELF UP TO THE WATERS."

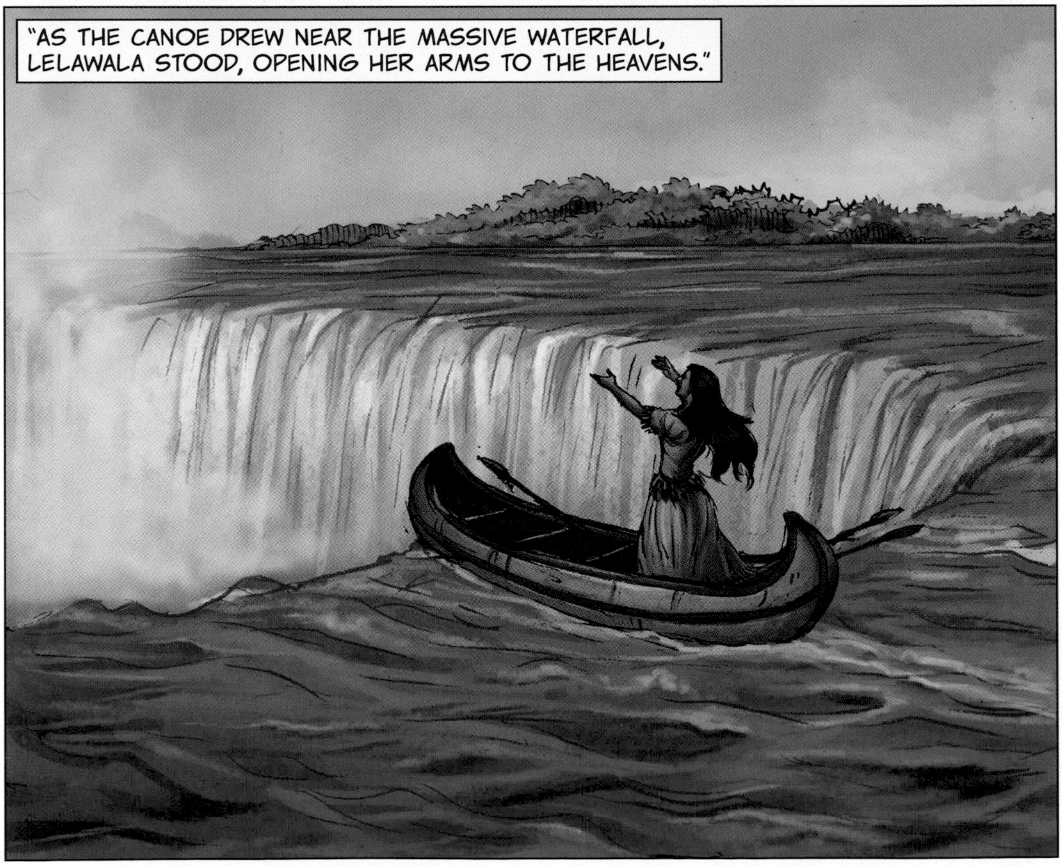
"AS THE CANOE DREW NEAR THE MASSIVE WATERFALL, LELAWALA STOOD, OPENING HER ARMS TO THE HEAVENS."

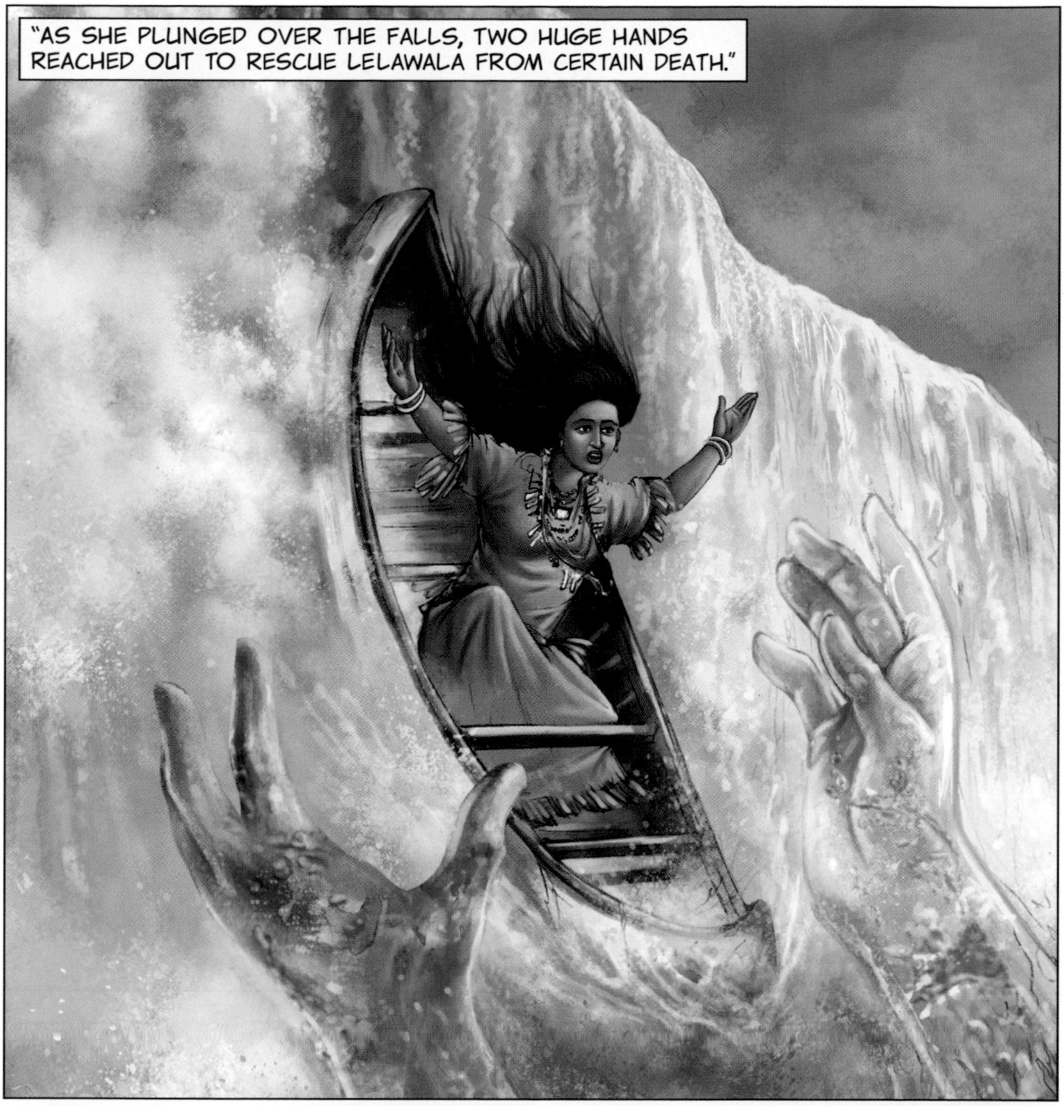
"AS SHE PLUNGED OVER THE FALLS, TWO HUGE HANDS REACHED OUT TO RESCUE LELAWALA FROM CERTAIN DEATH."

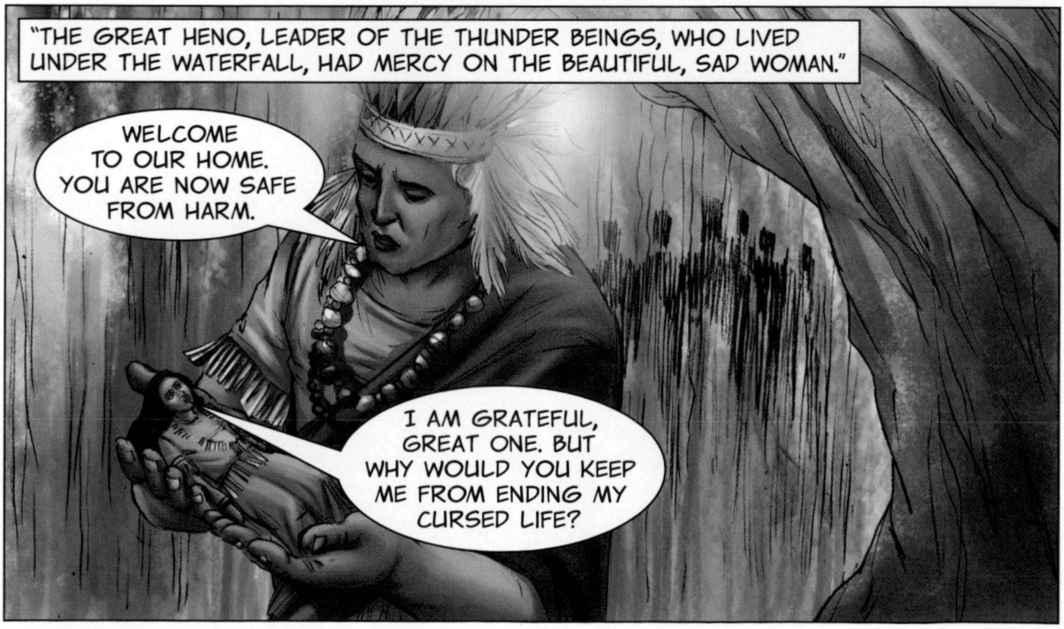
"THE GREAT HENO, LEADER OF THE THUNDER BEINGS, WHO LIVED UNDER THE WATERFALL, HAD MERCY ON THE BEAUTIFUL, SAD WOMAN."
WELCOME TO OUR HOME. YOU ARE NOW SAFE FROM HARM.
I AM GRATEFUL, GREAT ONE. BUT WHY WOULD YOU KEEP ME FROM ENDING MY CURSED LIFE?

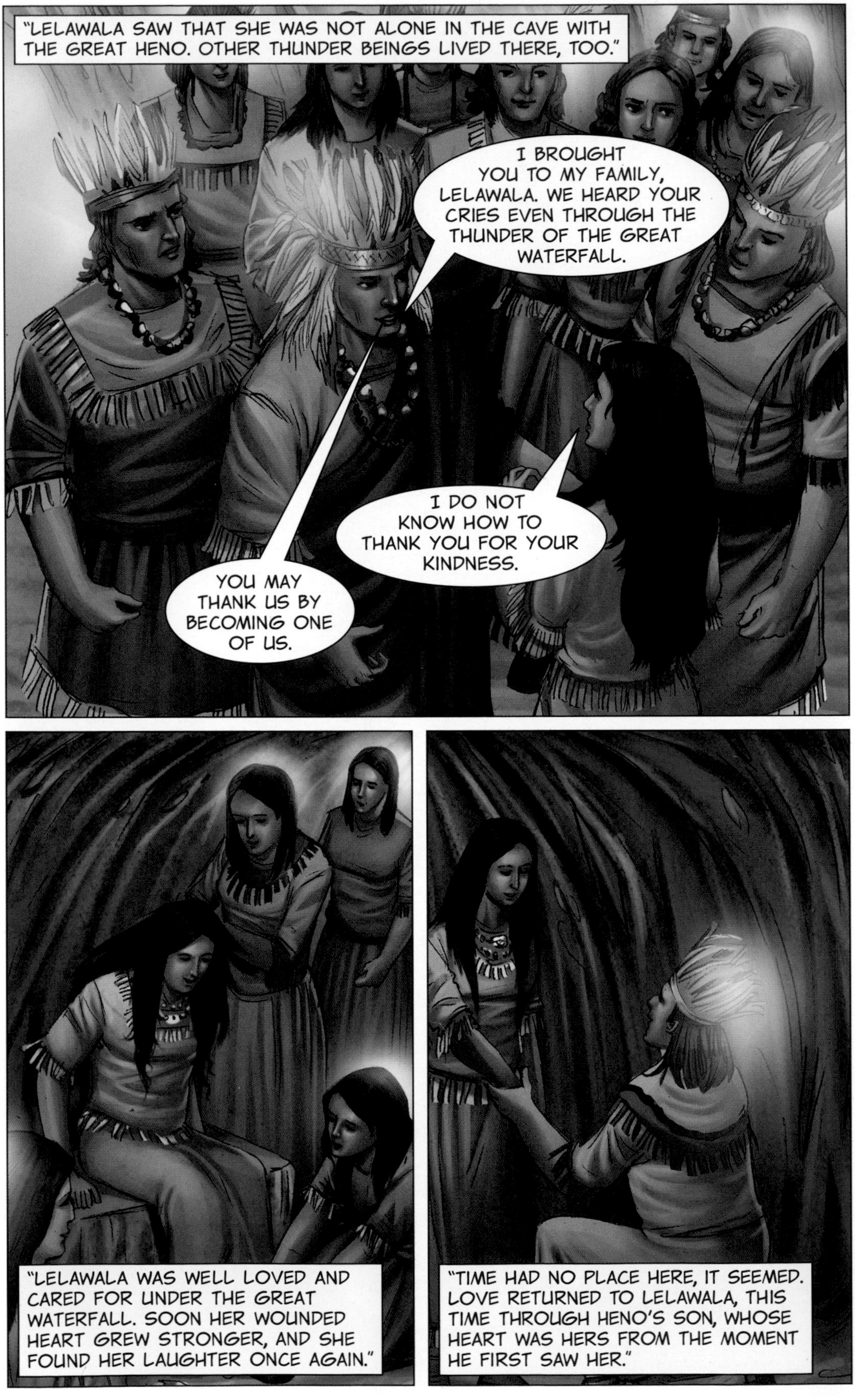
"LELAWALA SAW THAT SHE WAS NOT ALONE IN THE CAVE WITH THE GREAT HENO. OTHER THUNDER BEINGS LIVED THERE, TOO."
I BROUGHT YOU TO MY FAMILY, LELAWALA. WE HEARD YOUR CRIES EVEN THROUGH THE THUNDER OF THE GREAT WATERFALL.
I DO NOT KNOW HOW TO THANK YOU FOR YOUR KINDNESS.
YOU MAY THANK US BY BECOMING ONE OF US.
"LELAWALA WAS WELL LOVED AND CARED FOR UNDER THE GREAT WATERFALL. SOON HER WOUNDED HEART GREW STRONGER, AND SHE FOUND HER LAUGHTER ONCE AGAIN."
"TIME HAD NO PLACE HERE, IT SEEMED. LOVE RETURNED TO LELAWALA, THIS TIME THROUGH HENO'S SON, WHOSE HEART WAS HERS FROM THE MOMENT HE FIRST SAW HER."

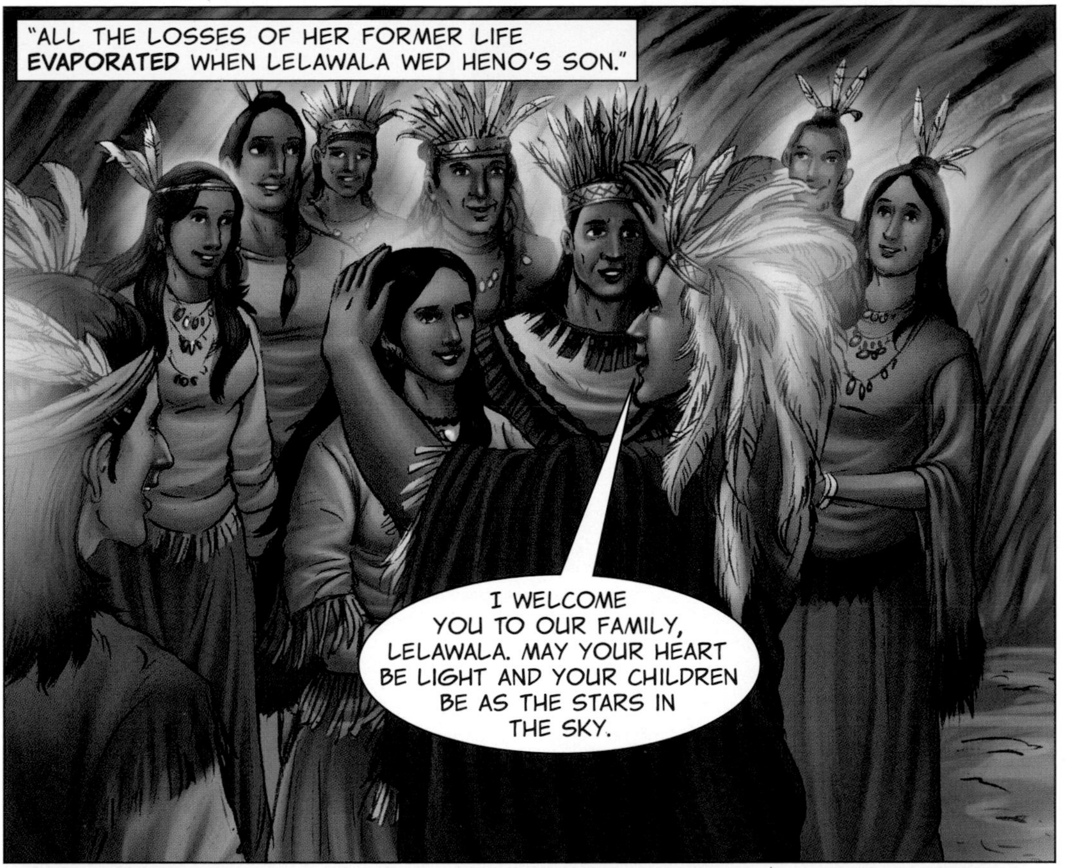
"ALL THE LOSSES OF HER FORMER LIFE EVAPORATED WHEN LELAWALA WED HENO'S SON."
I WELCOME YOU TO OUR FAMILY, LELAWALA. MAY YOUR HEART BE LIGHT AND YOUR CHILDREN BE AS THE STARS IN THE SKY.

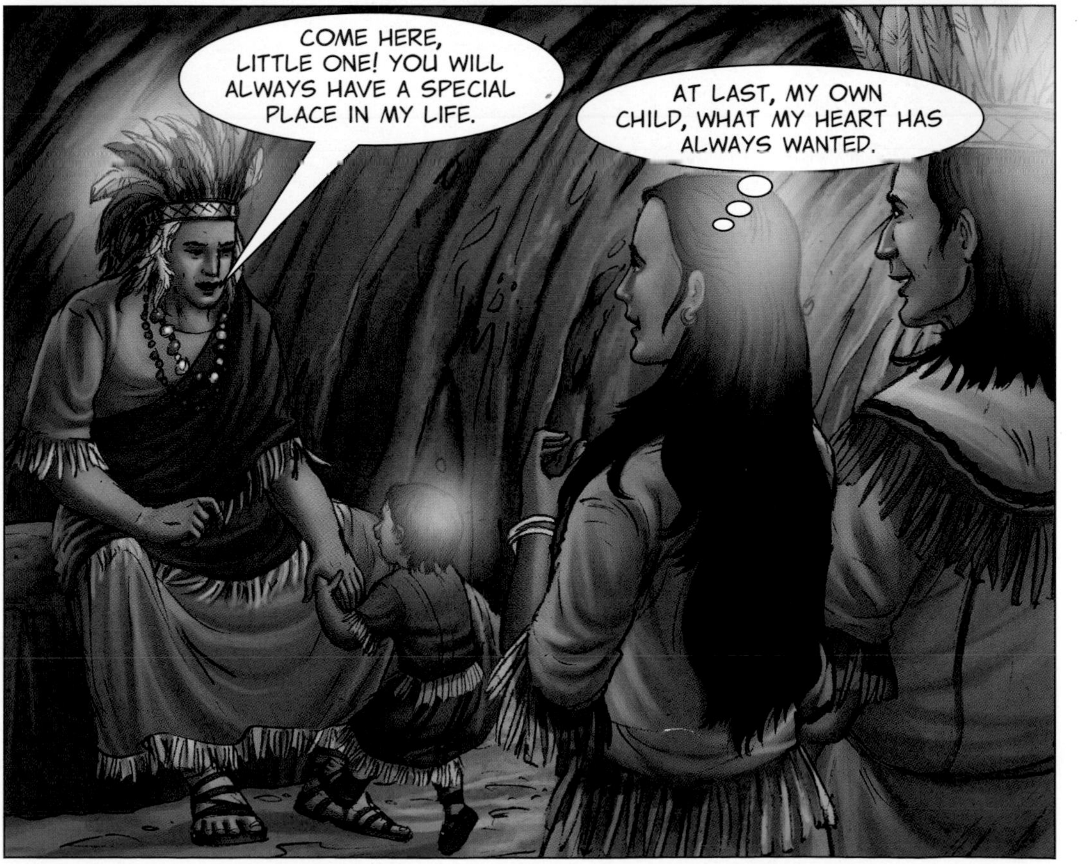
COME HERE, LITTLE ONE! YOU WILL ALWAYS HAVE A SPECIAL PLACE IN MY LIFE.
AT LAST, MY OWN CHILD, WHAT MY HEART HAS ALWAYS WANTED.

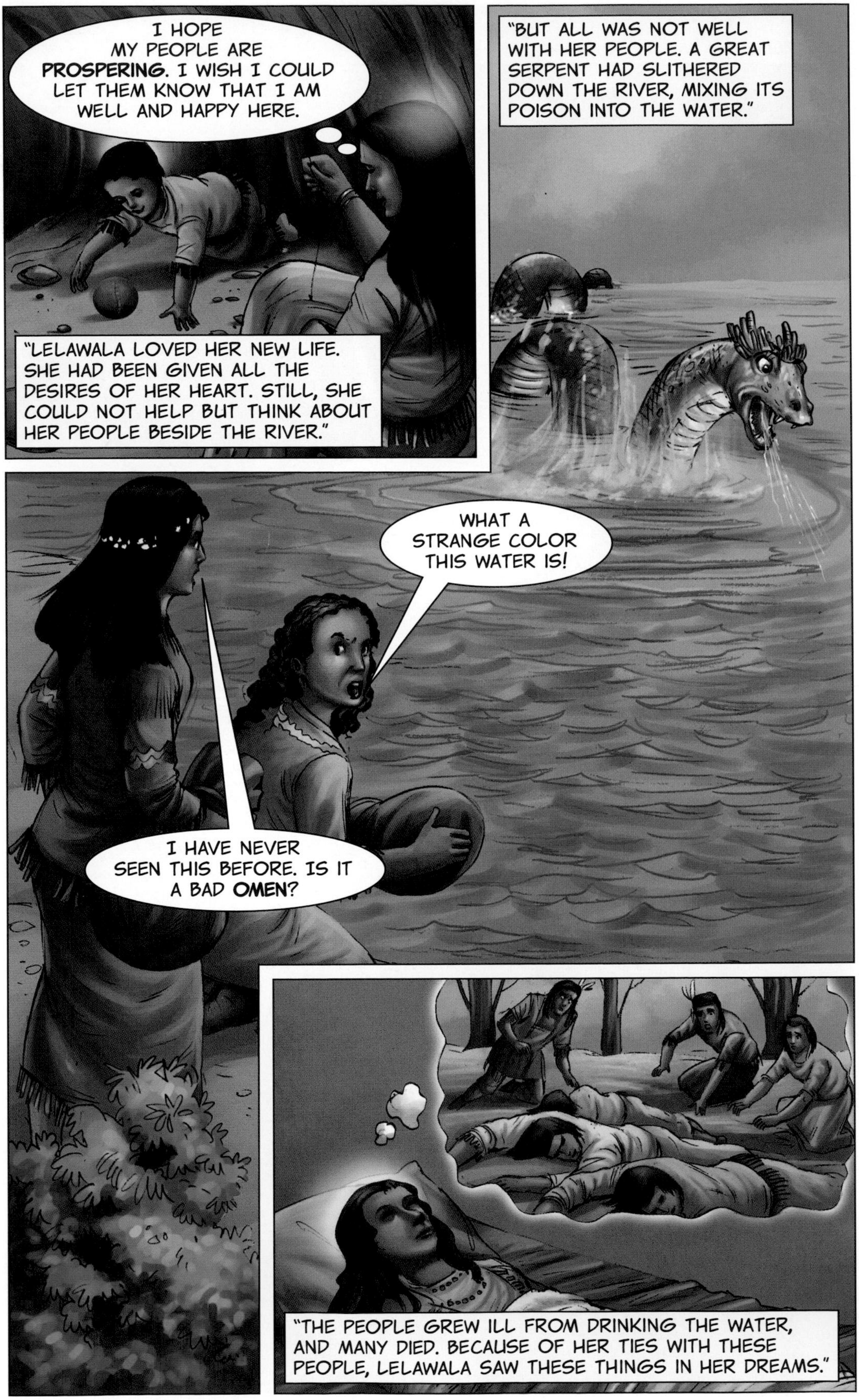
I HOPE MY PEOPLE ARE PROSPERING. I WISH I COULD LET THEM KNOW THAT I AM WELL AND HAPPY HERE.
"LELAWALA LOVED HER NEW LIFE. SHE HAD BEEN GIVEN ALL THE DESIRES OF HER HEART. STILL, SHE COULD NOT HELP BUT THINK ABOUT HER PEOPLE BESIDE THE RIVER."
"BUT ALL WAS NOT WELL WITH HER PEOPLE. A GREAT SERPENT HAD SLITHERED DOWN THE RIVER, MIXING ITS POISON INTO THE WATER."
WHAT A STRANGE COLOR THIS WATER IS!
I HAVE NEVER SEEN THIS BEFORE. IS IT A BAD OMEN?
"THE PEOPLE GREW ILL FROM DRINKING THE WATER, AND MANY DIED. BECAUSE OF HER TIES WITH THESE PEOPLE, LELAWALA SAW THESE THINGS IN HER DREAMS."

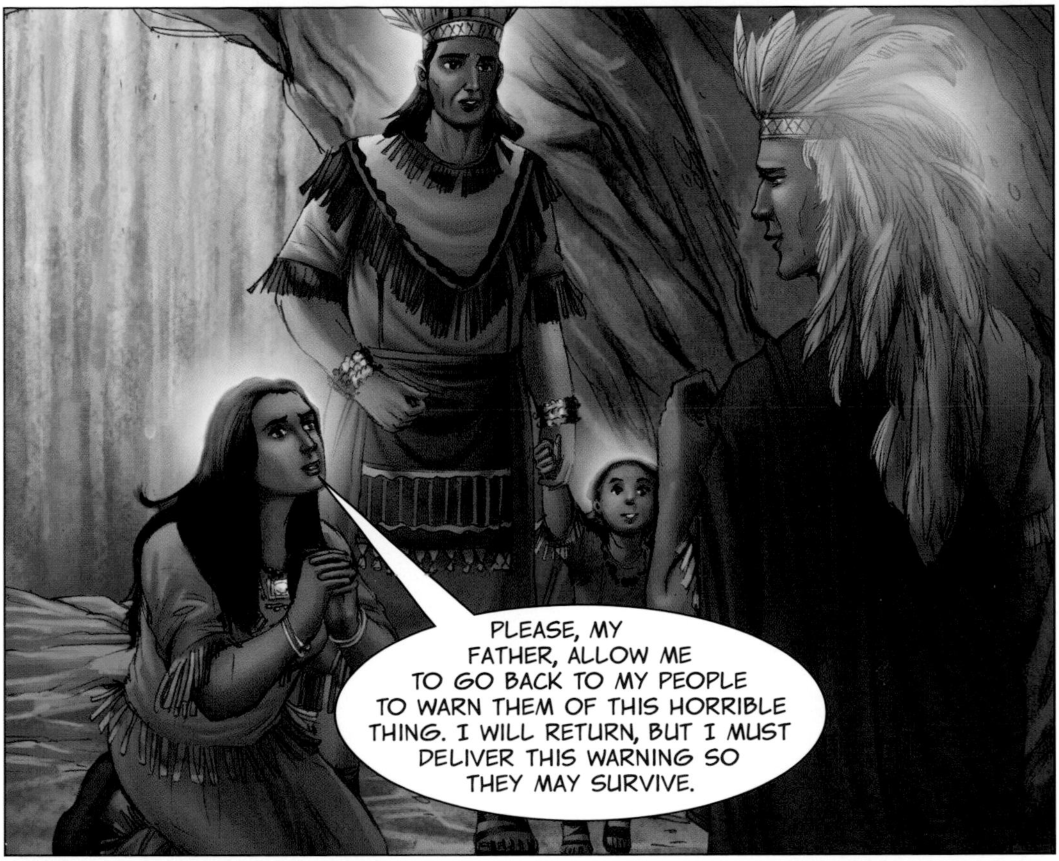
PLEASE, MY FATHER, ALLOW ME TO GO BACK TO MY PEOPLE TO WARN THEM OF THIS HORRIBLE THING. I WILL RETURN, BUT I MUST DELIVER THIS WARNING SO THEY MAY SURVIVE.

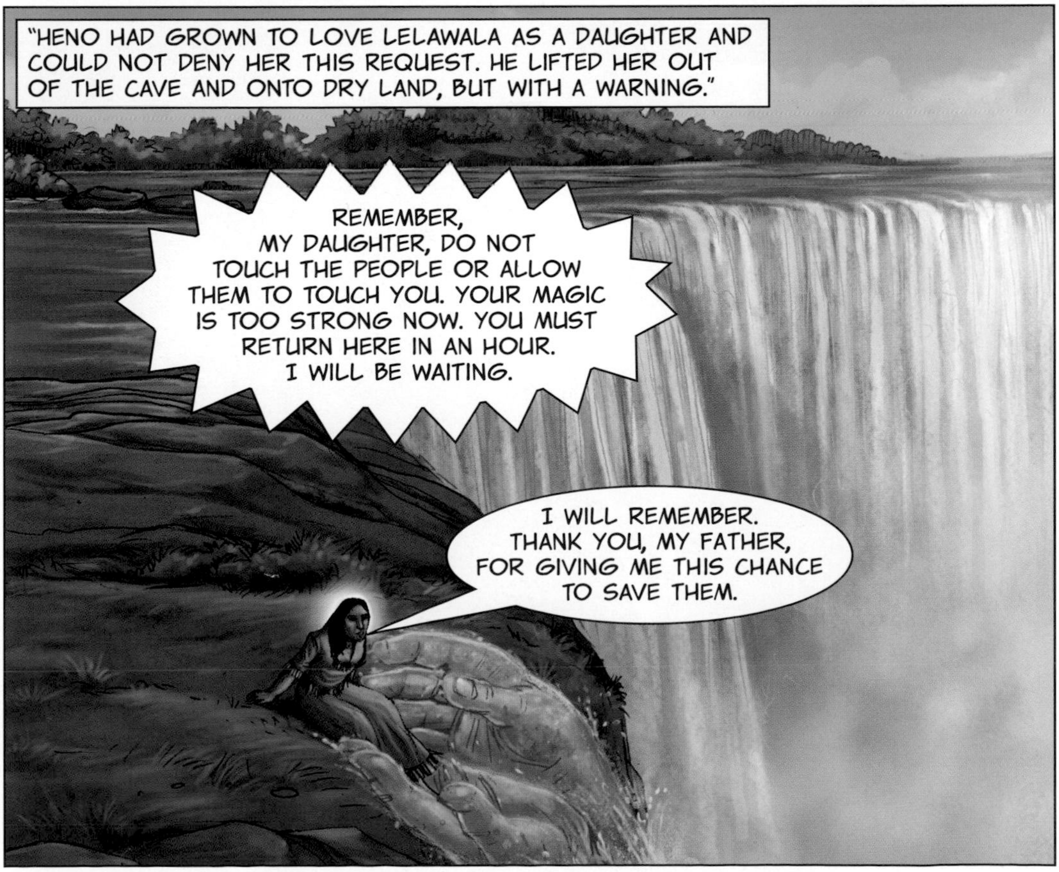
"HENO HAD GROWN TO LOVE LELAWALA AS A DAUGHTER AND COULD NOT DENY HER THIS REQUEST. HE LIFTED HER OUT OF THE CAVE AND ONTO DRY LAND, BUT WITH A WARNING."
REMEMBER, MY DAUGHTER, DO NOT TOUCH THE PEOPLE OR ALLOW THEM TO TOUCH YOU. YOUR MAGIC IS TOO STRONG NOW. YOU MUST RETURN HERE IN AN HOUR. I WILL BE WAITING.
I WILL REMEMBER. THANK YOU, MY FATHER, FOR GIVING ME THIS CHANCE TO SAVE THEM.

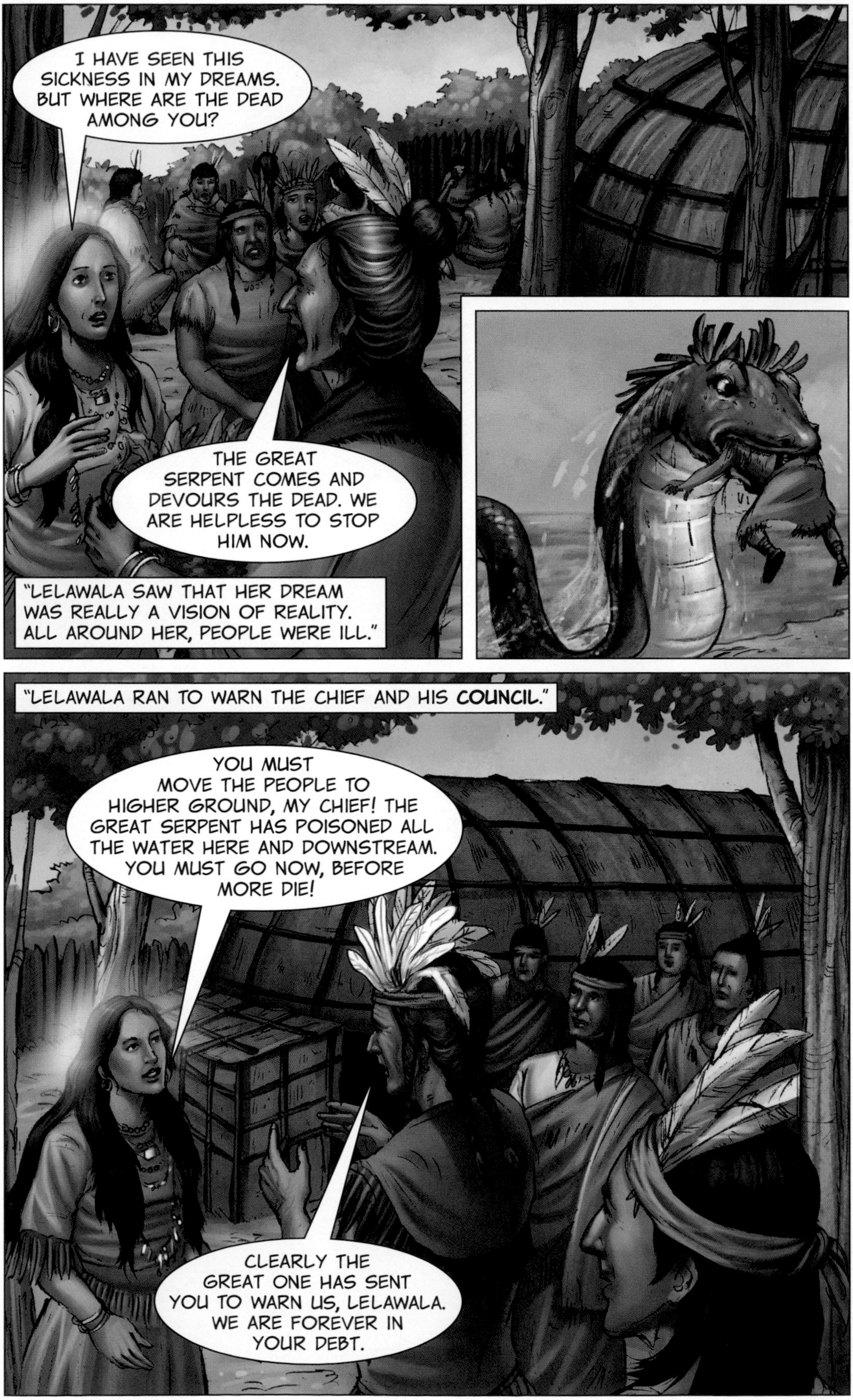
I HAVE SEEN THIS SICKNESS IN MY DREAMS. BUT WHERE ARE THE DEAD AMONG YOU?
THE GREAT SERPENT COMES AND DEVOURS THE DEAD. WE ARE HELPLESS TO STOP HIM NOW.
"LELAWALA SAW THAT HER DREAM WAS REALLY A VISION OF REALITY. ALL AROUND HER, PEOPLE WERE ILL."
"LELAWALA RAN TO WARN THE CHIEF AND HIS **COUNCIL**."
YOU MUST MOVE THE PEOPLE TO HIGHER GROUND, MY CHIEF! THE GREAT SERPENT HAS POISONED ALL THE WATER HERE AND DOWNSTREAM. YOU MUST GO NOW, BEFORE MORE DIE!
CLEARLY THE GREAT ONE HAS SENT YOU TO WARN US, LELAWALA. WE ARE FOREVER IN YOUR DEBT.

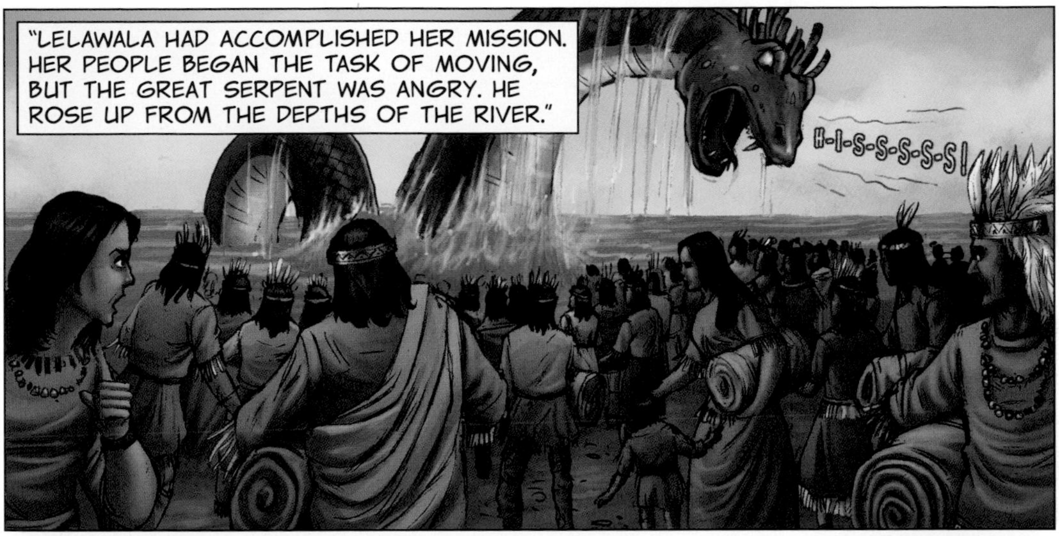
"LELAWALA HAD ACCOMPLISHED HER MISSION. HER PEOPLE BEGAN THE TASK OF MOVING, BUT THE GREAT SERPENT WAS ANGRY. HE ROSE UP FROM THE DEPTHS OF THE RIVER."
H-I-S-S-S-S-S!

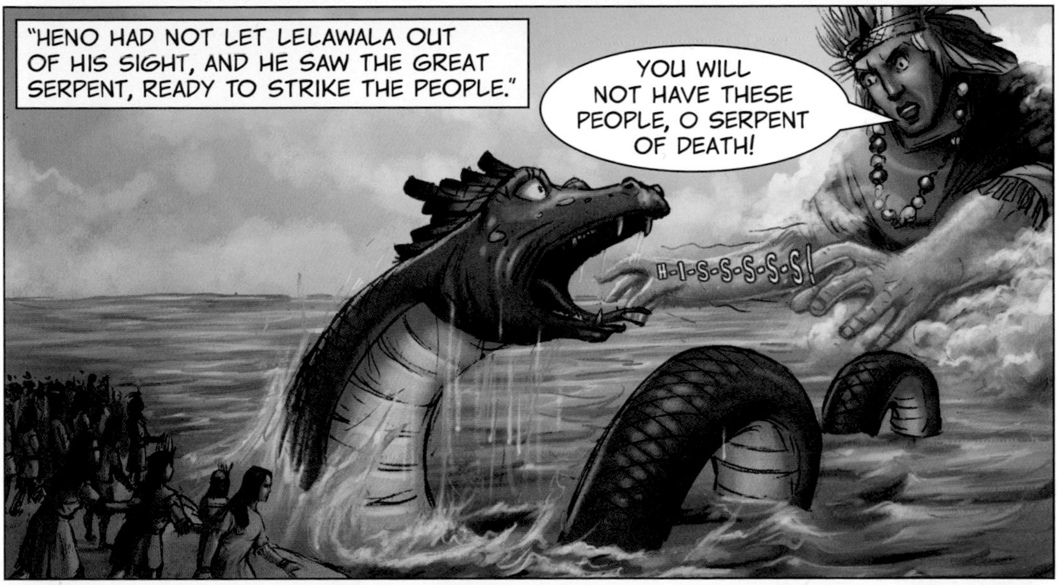
"HENO HAD NOT LET LELAWALA OUT OF HIS SIGHT, AND HE SAW THE GREAT SERPENT, READY TO STRIKE THE PEOPLE."
YOU WILL NOT HAVE THESE PEOPLE, O SERPENT OF DEATH!
H-I-S-S-S-S-S!

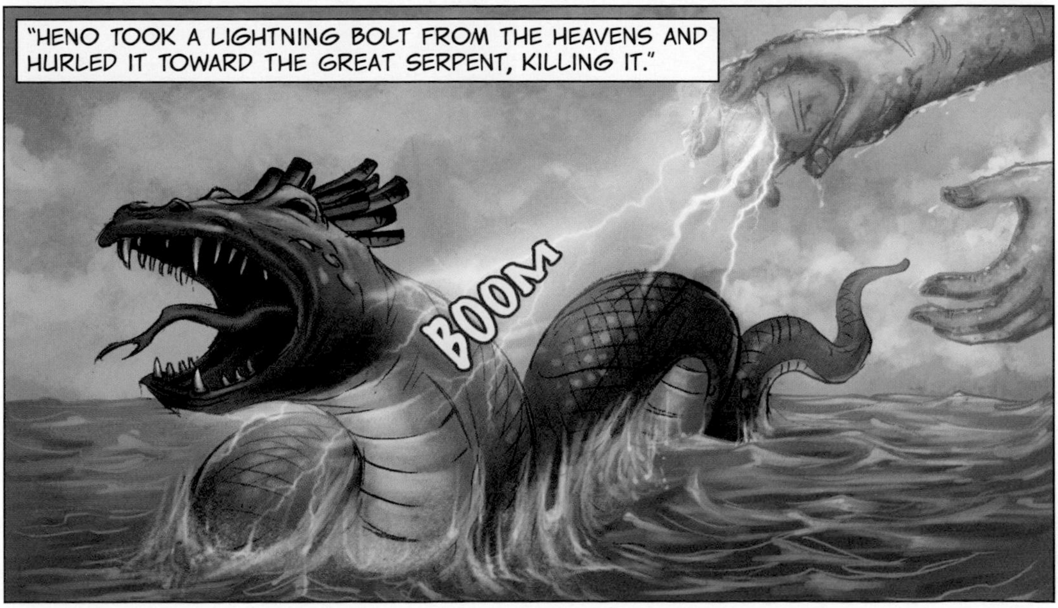
"HENO TOOK A LIGHTNING BOLT FROM THE HEAVENS AND HURLED IT TOWARD THE GREAT SERPENT, KILLING IT."
BOOM

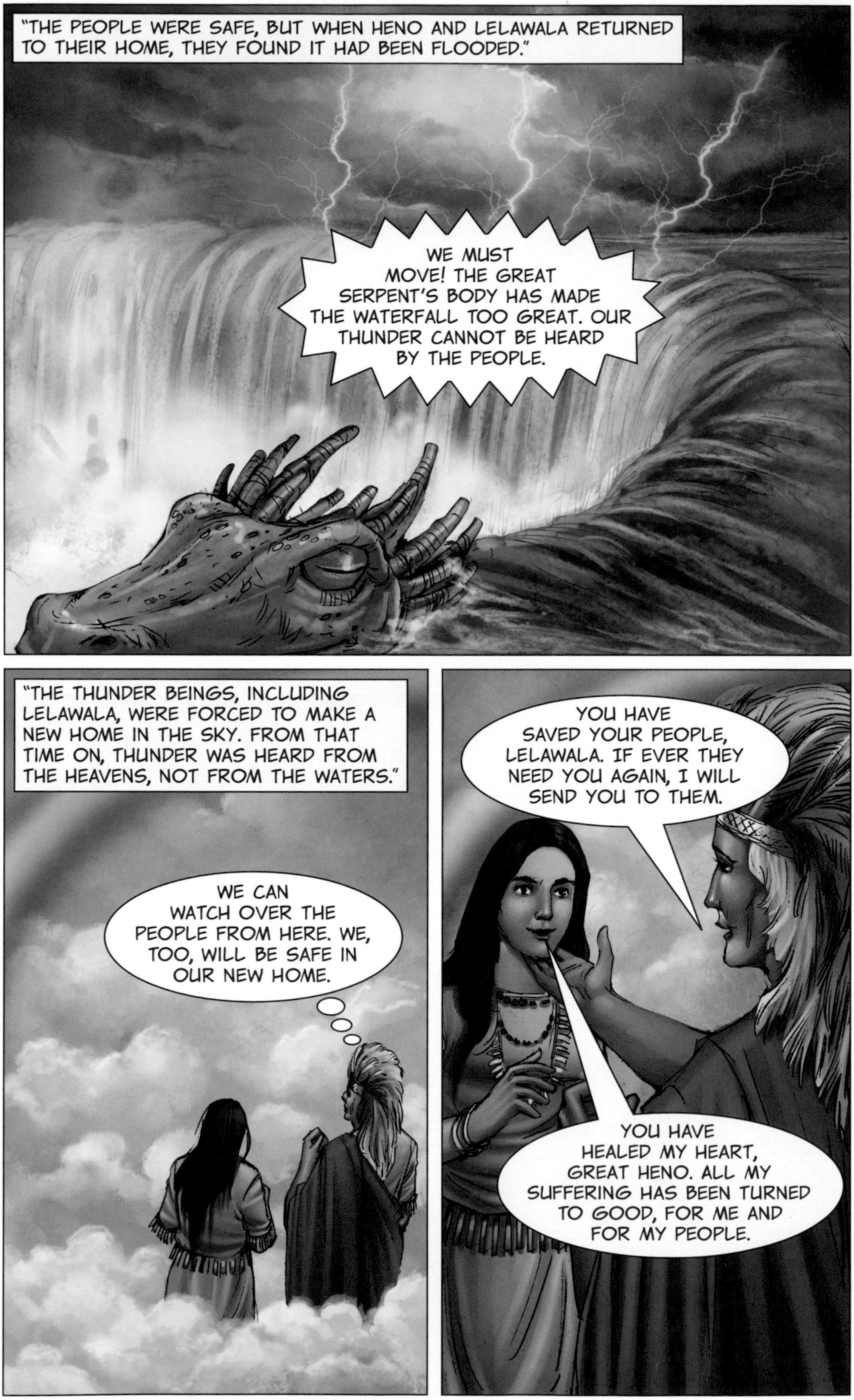
"THE PEOPLE WERE SAFE, BUT WHEN HENO AND LELAWALA RETURNED TO THEIR HOME, THEY FOUND IT HAD BEEN FLOODED."
WE MUST MOVE! THE GREAT SERPENT'S BODY HAS MADE THE WATERFALL TOO GREAT. OUR THUNDER CANNOT BE HEARD BY THE PEOPLE.
"THE THUNDER BEINGS, INCLUDING LELAWALA, WERE FORCED TO MAKE A NEW HOME IN THE SKY. FROM THAT TIME ON, THUNDER WAS HEARD FROM THE HEAVENS, NOT FROM THE WATERS."
WE CAN WATCH OVER THE PEOPLE FROM HERE. WE, TOO, WILL BE SAFE IN OUR NEW HOME.
YOU HAVE SAVED YOUR PEOPLE, LELAWALA. IF EVER THEY NEED YOU AGAIN, I WILL SEND YOU TO THEM.
YOU HAVE HEALED MY HEART, GREAT HENO. ALL MY SUFFERING HAS BEEN TURNED TO GOOD, FOR ME AND FOR MY PEOPLE.

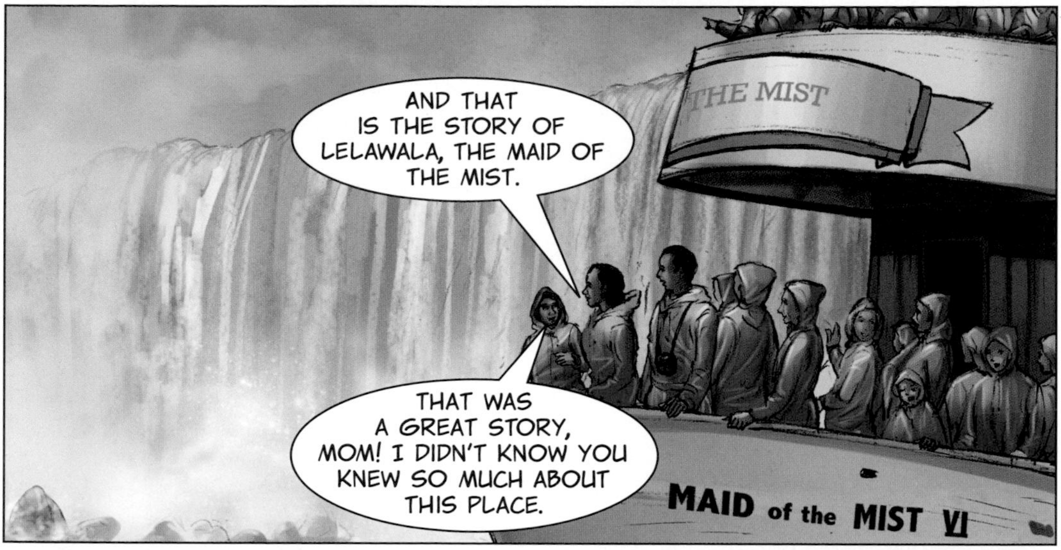
THE MIST
AND THAT IS THE STORY OF LELAWALA, THE MAID OF THE MIST.
THAT WAS A GREAT STORY, MOM! I DIDN'T KNOW YOU KNEW SO MUCH ABOUT THIS PLACE.
MAID of the MIST VI

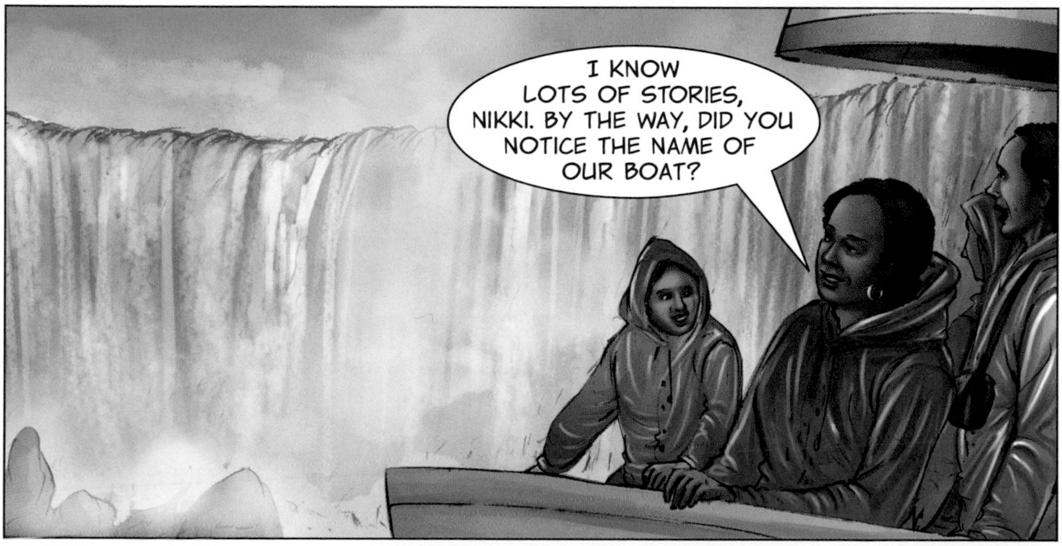
I KNOW LOTS OF STORIES, NIKKI. BY THE WAY, DID YOU NOTICE THE NAME OF OUR BOAT?

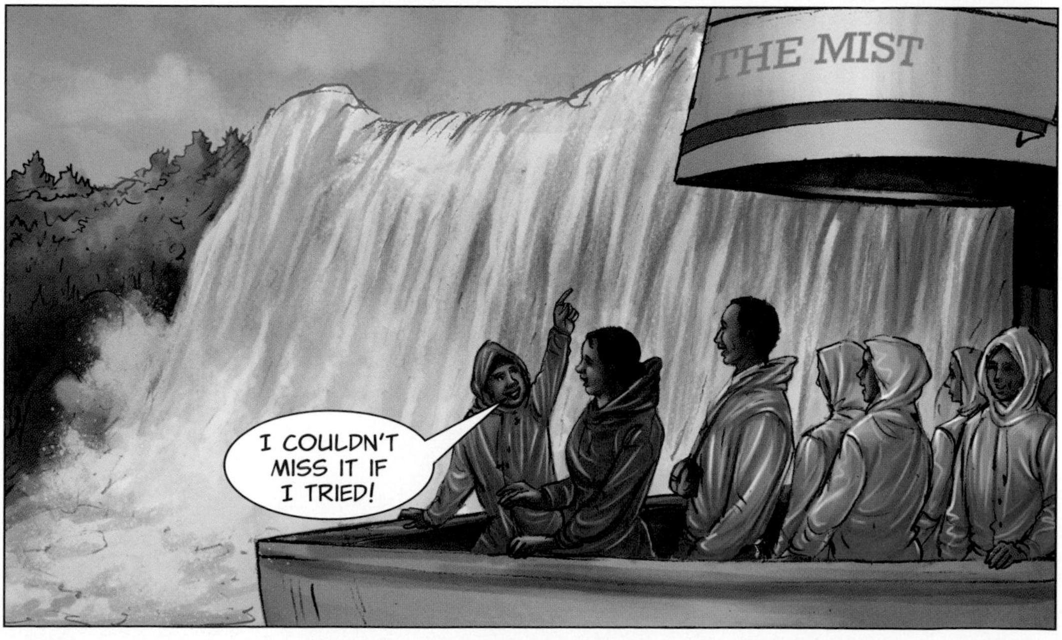
THE MIST
I COULDN'T MISS IT IF I TRIED!

More Iroquois Legends

- **How Fire Came to the Six Nations**
Three Arrows, son of the chief, was eager for his dream **fast**,
which would mark his entrance into manhood and show
him the animal that would be his special guardian. After five
dreamless days and nights, Three Arrows was starving, weak,
and worried. If he had no dream tonight, he would have to
return to his people without a guardian. He cried out to the
Great Spirit, begging for his dream to come. That night, a
huge bear appeared to him, giving him not only a guardian,
but also announcing Three Arrows would be taking a gift to
his people. In his dream, he saw two trees rubbing violently
against each other. Soon, a cloud of smoke appeared. Then
a flame ignited. When Three Arrows awoke, he found two
sticks and rubbed them together. Nothing happened at first;
but after much patience and effort, he saw a wisp of smoke.
Then a spark glowed. He had been given the gift of fire to
share with his people.

- **The Origin of the Pleiades (Seven Sisters Constellation)**
Long ago, hunters went in search of new hunting grounds.
Soon they came to a large lake filled with fish. The area
also held squirrels, bears, and chestnut trees. The hunters
built lodges there and brought their entire tribe to the new
grounds. After months of planting, growing, and harvesting,
the late fall brought a time of idleness. Eight children of the
tribe grew bored. They began to meet every day to dance
to break up the boredom. A wise old man came out of the
woods one day to warn the children to stop dancing before
evil came to them, but they ignored him. Soon thereafter,
they would rather dance than eat. One day as they danced,
they began to rise into the sky. Far up in the air, one of the
boys looked back to Earth and immediately fell. The others
kept rising and became the Pleiades. Every time a falling star
is seen, the people are reminded of the boy who looked back.

Glossary

barren (BER-en) Unable to have children.

canoe (kuh-NOO) A light, narrow boat that is pointed at both ends and that is moved through the water by paddling.

council (KOWN-sul) A group of people called together to discuss or settle questions.

evaporated (ih-VA-puh-rayt-ed) Vanished into the air.

fast (FAST) Choosing to go without food.

grieving (GREE-ving) Feeling great sorrow or distress.

inconsolable (in-kun-SOH-luh-bel) Unable to be comforted or cheered up.

longhouse (LONG-hows) A long, narrow, single-room building made by certain Native American groups.

medicine man (MEH-duh-sun MAN) A person who Native Americans believe to have close contact with the spirit world and to have the power to cure sickness.

neutral (NOO-trul) On neither side of an argument or of a war.

omen (OH-men) A happening that is believed to be a warning or sign of a future event.

Ongiara (on-gee-AR-ah) A small local tribe of the Iroquois people who lived in the region around the Niagara River in upstate New York and Ontario, Canada.

prospering (PROS-pur-ing) Being successful.

sacrifice (SA-kruh-fys) Something that has been given up for a belief.

smudge sticks (SMUJ STIKS) Small bundles, usually made of white sage, that, when burned, create a smoke believed to cleanse evil spirits.

spirit (SPEER-ut) A being whose existence cannot be explained by known laws of nature.

Index

Websites

Due to the changing nature of Internet links, PowerKids Press has developed an online list of websites related to the subject of this book. This site is updated regularly. Please use this link to access the list:

www.powerkidslinks.com/jggs/maid/